When's It MY Turn?

A Collection of Short Stories (and Temper Tantrums)

MELISSA RIXON, CHRISTI MCGUIRE, AND TERI MIRIKITANI

TRI SOLUTIONS LLC

DEDICATION

We dedicate this book to our husbands and children
for their endless love and support on this journey.

CONTENTS

"It's the moms of this nation—single, married, widowed—
who really hold this country together. We're the mothers,
we're the wives, we're the grandmothers, we're the big
sisters, we're the little sisters, we're the daughters.
You know it's true, don't you? You're the ones
who always have to do a little more."

—Ann Romney

INTRODUCTION

Two years ago, in an adorable café, three friends met for brunch and, in an unusual turn of events, felt compelled to just SPILL IT.

It was sort of like a party. The one where everyone wears yoga pants and the guests are cranky and sad.

"I have these dreams and this desire to *be* somebody, but my life is dominated by these little people I brought into the world, and I, personally, am going nowhere!"

"Do you ever feel like life will never be about you again?" we asked one another. "If you had the chance to do something right now, just for you, what would it be? Do you even know?"

"By the time we do get our lives back, will there be anything left? Or will we be all dried up and shrunken and gross and fresh out of ideas, just corralling whatever brain cells we have left into keeping us from drooling?"

Yeah . . . we're not dramatic at all.

Amped up on anguish, panic, and caffeine, over a table littered with half-eaten fruit and cold eggs, we carried on like desperate gamblers. Each time one of us would throw out a concern, another one of us would see it and raise it. In the end, all our hopes, dreams, fears, and marbles were rolling around before us among the toast and grits.

But then, something magical happened. We were glowing with happiness. We were thrilled to know we were not the only grapes withering away to raisins on the vine. If you've got to be a raisin, you might as well have raisin friends. Like the Golden Girls! Right?

Better yet, in that moment we decided that we weren't going to keep on withering. We were going to defy all laws of nature and come back to LIFE. It was miraculous. Magic swirled around us like all those dusty, sparkly clouds you see in cartoons. We could feel it in the air.

"I'm going to be a writer!" one of us squealed.

"I'm going to get my life coaching business off the ground!" another piped in.

"I'm going to finish up the online courses I've been writing and get started on my consulting firm," the last of us followed up.

> To be a mom means your life and schedule are dictated by everyone else's bookings and obligations.
> It means you're on call, on the clock, on the line, on the horn, and on the road.

We walked out of that cafe, lassos in hand, ready to wrangle all the dreams we'd been conjuring in the lonely pastures of our living rooms and make them a reality. We were ready to carve out our space in the day. In our lives. In the world and even beyond.

The rest of that day, signs were everywhere. *This is your path!* they seemed to say. *This is your destiny!* It was so real we couldn't have ignored it if we'd wanted to. We wanted to bottle it. Use it! Drink it all up! This elixir of passion! This sweet nectar of promise!

With more spirit than ten thousand Tony Robbinses, we were going places. It was time. It was ours. We just had to take it, that's all.

But then on our way to take it, hurling sixty miles an hour toward our goals, we'd realize we ran out of toilet paper and have to go to the grocery store. Or our mother would call to complain about her knee acting up again. Or a kid would have a fever and be home from school three days in a row. Slowly, that elixir of passion began to taste a little bit like milk of magnesia. The sweet nectar of promise went rancid, and that blasted sparkly magic cloud turned into a flimsy, pathetic wisp of smoke hovering in the corner.

We were back to being sad.

It was just life, as we knew it at the moment.

If you had asked us what was lighting our fire, what was driving us, or what was keeping us up at night with excitement, we'd have looked at you like that little emoji with its closed mouth turned up to one side. It's the look that says, "Well . . ." and then that's it. That's all it says.

Our job descriptions for motherhood, at this moment in time, consist of 839,000 things, which all can boil down to one: *be available*. Period. It sounds so free, doesn't it? Just be available! Be open. Be *un*-booked. Yet, there's nothing quite as binding.

To be available means to be everything.

It means your life and schedule are dictated by everyone else's bookings and obligations. It means you're on call, on the clock, on the line, on the horn, and on the road. All while you squeeze the bits of your own needs into the hairline fractures in the itinerary.

If you've ever found yourself crying out to a pile of laundry, "When's it gonna be about *me*?" . . . If you've ever chiseled away at your pot roast with maybe a little too much aggression and a white-knuckle grip on your carving knife while you holler, "Where is *my* space in the world?" . . . If you've ever punched that too big, king-sized feather pillow while stuffing it impossibly into that ridiculously too narrow pillowcase and screamed, "When's it MY turn?" . . . then this book is for you.

To be available means to be everything.

Because the answer to those questions came loud and clear and abrupt as an earthquake the day we returned to that little cafe. It was like God himself delivered the answers on stone tablets into our open Moses arms. That back corner table was our Mount Sinai, and we came down from there with direction clear as church bells.

Oh, now that would have been so helpful. But, in fact, we're kidding. There was no answer. There was no manual. There were no tablets, burning bushes, bells, ghosts, or creepy messages written in our burnt toast.

We did one simple thing. We vowed never to stop dreaming. We vowed never to stop sharing our dreams with each other. We vowed that even if we were eighty-nine and could barely see and were bumping into each other at brunch, we would keep the hope alive. Because feeling bled out and picked clean and tattered and torn is easier to tolerate with a hearty helping of hope, a bowl of good Southern grits, and your soul-sister friends who are just as imperfect as you are.

So if you're in need of a little hope or maybe just need to have a mother-sized fit, you've come to the right place.

There's a seat at this table for you.

—Melissa, Christi, and Teri

1

GLASS AND SCAFFOLDS

by Christi McGuire

My childhood was idyllic. It had all the things you might see in the opening of a perfect movie set in the country. The mom, the dad, the kids, the dog. The old, large farmhouse. Horses grazing in the pasture. The white picket fence.

We'd run amok in the yard while mom spent Sunday afternoons in the kitchen, piecing together a pot roast with careful trimmings and the vegetables she'd canned from our garden.

Sitting around our kitchen table, we'd wash it all down with her freshly-brewed iced tea and talk about the church service and plan our Mondays. The crisp breeze joined us through our farmhouse windows, fluttering the curtains my grandma had hand sewn, tickling us with its invisible fingers and invigorating us with the kind of energy you can only find in nature.

I can still feel that breeze. And if I steal a rare moment for myself and try hard enough, I can smell the freshly-baked chocolate chip cookies Mom would make after school. I can still see her making her own yogurt, wiping her hands on her apron to give me a clean hug after I'd gotten of the school bus and unloaded my backpack and my childish cares into her arms.

Then my sisters and I would race out to play on the metal, tottering swing set or play hide and seek in the hay lofts. Or chase the herd of sheep in the field or challenge one another on our Big Wheels.

Mom would call us inside as dusk crept in, corralling us all into the bathtub. With shiny, wet hair and squeaky-clean faces, we'd don our jammies and snuggle together on the front porch swing, listening to the crickets chirp and watching the stars begin to twinkle.

At the end of a long day of such adventure, I'd pretend we were just like the Ingalls family, settling into our own Little House on the Prairie and listening to Pa play his fiddle while Ma cross-stitched a tea towel, as Mary, Laura, and Carrie dutifully and lovingly played with one another. It all seemed right. And I knew this was exactly what I wanted in my own family someday. This perfection. This nostalgia.

Life was going to be like this snapshot of perfection I held captive in my memory.

But perfect things are made of glass—fragile and vulnerable.

On a flawless Sunday night, driving home from church, where Mom had played the piano and we had run around the church yard with friends, those perfect things shattered into dust with one question. "What would you do if your dad and I got divorced?" Mom asked.

And that's as far as the crispy memories and sweet smells of home will go.

I remember lightly dismissing my mom's question with all the disdain my child heart could muster, saying, "Well, you'd better not."

But ten-year-olds don't make the rules. Grown-ups do. And that Sunday night, our bellies still satiated from the day's pot roast and mom's homegrown vegetables, was the last night we were a whole family. He tucked us in our beds. He kissed us good-night. And the next morning . . . my dad was gone.

I tried to be strong. Twisted myself into a scaffold underneath my mother, who couldn't keep from falling apart, no matter how hard she tried not to. And then I expanded that scaffold under and around my younger sisters who suddenly seemed so little to me. I took up the duties expected of the oldest daughter and big sister. I washed dishes, folded laundry, vacuumed, made beds, picked up toys.

I became orderly, practical, and strong, keeping the pieces picked up and the façade of perfection nice and shiny for the onlookers. *Nothing to see, folks!* I wanted to scream as I stretched myself further to keep everyone from sinking.

This isn't gonna be so bad, I would tell myself, and I'd think of Margaret in Judy Blume's book, *Are You There God? It's Me, Margaret*, and how she got two Christmases out of a divorce. So how bad could it be?

I was proud of the way it didn't take me out at the knees. Oh, it almost did. Once, in the middle of English class, it certainly almost did, but my teacher reminded me to "buck up" and be grateful for a roof over my head and food on my table. So I fortified myself, did as I was told, bucked up, and carried on.

It almost did at church, when our friends stopped calling and were suddenly too busy to come around, making every attempt to dance around the real reason—a scarlet "D" on your church clothes makes you an uncomfortable friend. After all, reminders that bad things can happen to good people who show up every Sunday are unsettling. And unsettling things feel dangerous in circles built for safety.

So I learned.

I learned to be unaffected by divorce. I took all the shards and glassy dust and reformed myself with it. Perfect. Without scars or marks. And I went on to do all the life things. I got married. I cared for a home. I had little girls of my own.

And I was pretty proud of the way I'd managed to escape.

I'm an imperfect mom.

An imperfect wife.

An imperfect daughter and friend.

I'm imperfect.

And it feels good to live here in this place where I can admit it.

9

In an effort to guard us from life's let downs, I imposed impossible standards on my own marriage and on myself as a wife and mother. Because Ma Ingalls was my role model and example. And because when you've been through the horrors of divorce, how could you forgive yourself for putting your own kids through it? I was the grown-up now. The one who made the rules and kept things shipshape. Who handed out scripts and lists and blueprints and play books.

If everyone just follows my lead, then nobody gets hurt, I thought. I *clung* to that thought.

But then one day I pulled an empty ice cube tray out of the freezer. Suddenly, there they were. All the fragments of that former shattered life, which had burrowed through my soul, were now bursting forth, demolishing the perfect exterior I had so carefully constructed.

"How could you!" I screamed at my husband. I gulped between sobs. "You never put an empty ice cube tray in the freezer. You fill. it. up. And then you put it back!"

Then there were the things I couldn't put into words. Because they were the thoughts I'd sealed underneath myself the day I bucked up. *Because my dad did this. Just like this. Lazily put the empty ice cube tray in the freezer. And then he had an affair and cheated on my mom, which meant he cheated on us. So that means you might too. And I won't be able to handle it if I end up like my mom. Alone, raising these kids. Who will build a scaffold under me?*

And that outburst led to another one. And another one, until I realized that doing life as if nothing was wrong was—well, wrong. I hadn't remade myself perfect again. In fact, I was screwed up. *We* were screwed up. And maybe by a lot.

I had to recalibrate. Because all these little lives that happen together under our roofs can't be contained by our Master Plans. Life isn't a book you've read. It's a book you're writing. It's not a movie you've seen with strategic plot points and intentional conflicts; it's in chaotic disarray. It's in need of a mom, not a movie director. Because moms manage disarray, without believing they can eliminate it or even trying to. I had to learn to accept it. To live among it. To see the disorder and the arguments and the unmatched socks and call it home, trusting that just because it's messy doesn't mean the people inside it will think it's worthless and walk out.

Emily Griffin has a beautiful quote in her book, *Something Borrowed*: "I am learning that perfection isn't what matters. In fact, it's the very thing that can destroy you if you let it."

I'm living proof of that. The struggle for perfection in and of itself is imperfect and will take a sledge hammer to anything you build out of glass. And it would have destroyed me too if it hadn't been for a dozen amazing friends who have been there to say something as life-giving and uplifting as, "Me too. I'm hanging by a thread too. Most days. Most minutes. Most of the tiny milliseconds of my life are made of strings pulled by other people, and that makes me a mess. But let's be a mess together."

Together, we can cry over spilled milk, even though they say it's no use. Together, we can lament over dreams we let go like balloons, for the sake of our families. Together, we can revel in the *importance* of imperfect stories and remind each other to cry if you must but also laugh—laugh often and in spite of all the craziness this life throws at us. Together, we can ratchet ourselves into scaffolds and hold each other up.

Who am I? I'm an imperfect mom. An imperfect wife. An imperfect daughter and friend. I'm imperfect. And it feels good to live here in this place where I can admit it. It's one of the most critical things about who I've become.

Join me in this space where we are unorganized and unhinged and uninhibited by pretense. I'm a mess. I'm confused. And I refuse to pretend I have all the answers. Because I certainly don't. Instead, I prefer to pretend to fly to the moon where I can look down on all this with a sense of pride.

If you're feeling that same exhaustion of protecting glass things, then come cozy up. There's a better way to spend your time.

TEMPER TANTRUM

Toothpaste spit in the sink.

Because, of course, I want to clean up your spit

and a week's worth of dried Colgate.

2

TIME MACHINE

by Melissa Rixon

"So would you ever go back to your twenties?" one of us asked. I forget why, but it must have had something to do with our discussion questions. Our book club sat around an empty dessert plate. One we'd all shared because women our age don't dare eat an entire slab of cake alone.

Maybe I'd go back and eat more cake, I thought.

We waxed nostalgic for a while about rocket-hot metabolisms, stores of energy, and schedules that used to be full of . . . what?

What had we done with ourselves before we were moms?

On the way home, a little something stung? Ached? Longed? No. It wasn't that. It just *existed*. A pang was present that I couldn't ignore. I felt a need to address that question in a real way.

Would I go back to my twenties?

It's tempting at first, thinking of that figure, that sense of style. The version of you who doesn't know what's coming is the one with all the audacity to daydream about the future: power lunches, important jobs, and fancy things.

I imagined a time machine of sorts and what it might be like to step out of such a contraption and interrupt my Twenty Something Self while she's crawling out of a tanning bed. What would I say to her? What would she think of me? My imagination played the footage . . .

I give her a second to get herself together and get over the shock and awe of seeing her forty-year-old face. Then I slap her for tanning and tell her it's her own stupid fault before we go back to her apartment and chat.

We walk in, and the scent of cheap, pear-scented, body spray socks me in the memory tanks, and I immediately want to crawl into my old bed and take a nap. Gretyl, my little, floppy, spotted dachshund, who ate my retainer and was never fully potty trained, licks me to death and then pees on the carpet. I well with tears because, *man,* I loved that dog anyway.

Twenty-Something Self happily cleans it up and offers me a Dr. Pepper. I marvel at her lack of stress and imagine dog pee on Forty-Year-Old Self's expensive area rugs and shudder. I stick to my unsweetened tea and catch myself thinking, with certain pride, *I'll bet she ate French fries today.*

We sit on the couch, and she hugs a pillow. I know what she doesn't say—that holding her pillow allows her to relax and breathe without her stomach sucked in or her shoulders held straight. The back-breaking work of appearing to be perfect is tiring, and that pillow relieves her.

I tell her, "Ask me anything you want," and she rattles off questions while youth dances around in the shine of her eyes. Questions about who I marry and how much money we have. Where do I live and in what kind of house? How many kids do I have, and do I ever do the *writing thing?*

I answer the questions like I might sort jelly beans by color. Without much thinking, because the questions aren't thoughtful. *Am I happy? Fulfilled? Is life still exciting?* These are the questions I would ask now.

The youth in her eyes slows the dance. I'm ruining it, probably bumming her out, and so I immediately stand up to go.

I feel her gaze heavy on my back, sizing me up. "So nothing works out?" she cries, a ribbon of fear curling around her voice. "This is all there is to *me?*"

I'm not offended. Not really. Maybe the idea of dreams not coming true is the reason we can't travel time.

I turn around slowly, face-to-face with myself. This girl who dreamed of New York, not the 'burbs.

I smile.

It's a motherly smile, which of course it is. A smile that says, "There, there." Barely a whisper, I say, "Yeah. This is you. This is me. This is . . . *us.* This is what you look like as a woman. And maybe it's scary, but it doesn't happen all at once, which is good. You hardly even feel it until you see an old picture, and sometimes that old picture makes you a little bit sad. But this face . . . the lines here, here, and here are just chapters in the novel you write. And if you look closely, they're right where you smile, and around the corners of your eyes from when the smiles are genuine. And here's the good news. They're genuine *most of the time.*

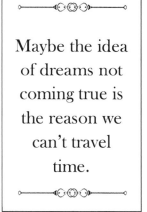

Maybe the idea of dreams not coming true is the reason we can't travel time.

"You're an elementary school room mom and a Girl Scout leader. Then there's the book club, which sounds boring, but it's not. A subdivision house is what you call home, and you park a blue minivan in the driveway while you yell at three kids for putting gum in the ashtray and leaving cups to leak into the cup holders—but what does it matter . . . that's the reason you bought the uncool car in the first place.

"When you're pregnant, you'll gain fifty-one pounds, and then lose it in time to get pregnant again. You'll do that three times before you settle into a weight permanently ten pounds too much. You'll only wear makeup when you absolutely have to and average three days between shampoos.

"These hips? Well . . . three babies. This is just what hips do. And they were built to do it, so stop crying. It's okay. These hips carried and brought three human beings, punctuated with details like fingernails and eyelashes, screaming and slippery into the open arms of a wonderful man who loves you and your hips.

"There is so much that isn't what you thought. Sometimes, that will bite a little bit. It will feel like disappointment, and I know disappointment is tough. There are days and days when you'll pine for a little more adventure . . . energy . . . a little more freedom to seek out some thrills. There's the mom clothes, the extra ten pounds, the wrinkles, and the sticky cup holders. It probably sounds like a terrible mess. And so many days it's exactly that. One out-of-whack, nearly catastrophic, life-on-a-boiler-plate kind of hot mess. And I have off days when I look back and wonder if maybe I've failed you.

"But then, your son will win awards for things like academics or something really important like *being kind*. Your daughter will play so hard at soccer she nearly passes out. And even though she doesn't score, she keeps trying, and her wanting to, trying to, and not giving up gets to you. And suddenly, right in the middle of a soccer field, you'll realize you're crying like a crazy lady. Your baby will say a first word or take a first step and—even though this planet is full of billions of human beings walking and talking—to you that moment will feel like a miracle. Like it's never been done in the history of time.

"There is so much to be proud of. Pride that makes you come completely undone in public and overshare on Facebook (that's a thing I'm glad wasn't around at your age). Because you will never feel so proud as you do of your children. Never.

"People will try to tell you how much you'll love your kids because they want you to understand, but you can't. You know you'll love them 'a lot,' but you can't begin to comprehend what it *is*. How powerful and consuming and vulnerable it is.

"And, no. You've never been to Germany or New Zealand or Spain, and while you start to do the *writing thing*, you doubt yourself constantly. You've never seen Bon Jovi in concert or hiked the Pacific Coast Trail or skied the Alps or seen the northern lights. But, oh, the things you *have* done. So many beautiful things. Things you've tried and seen and places you've been and people you've met. Things that will turn your heart into something like the center of a cinnamon bun.

"Surprises await you. And surprises they should be, so I'll go. I'll leave you to it, so you can go get your belly button pierced.

Although, I'll warn you, your daughter will ask you about that scar one day, and you will feel most uncomfortable telling her the truth about it. Because she's very conservative, that one, and can make you feel like you're answering to your mother.

"In one parting thought or word of advice, don't be discouraged. Don't give up on those dreams, kid. It's all the things you haven't done that keeps youth dancing in the shine of your eyes. And, yes, you still have that. Even at forty."

THINGS NO ONE TELLS YOU

The dog, the delivery man, and the door-to-door salesman will all make your Most Wanted hit list if they wake your napping infant.

Babies either smell amazing or foul. There is no such thing as an in-between, sort-of-okay smelling baby.

You are going to cheer for any and all gas you can work out of your baby.

Swim diapers are a thing. They work by pushing the poop up your baby's back into her floatation device.

When your kid poops in the resort swimming pool, they close it down for cleaning. This makes you very unpopular. The swim diaper does nothing to prevent this from happening.

Just when you think it can't get any worse than Play-Doh, they will make something like Moon Sand. Don't ask what can be worse than Moon Sand. We don't want to know the answer to this.

3

ECHOES AND EMBERS

by Teri Mirikitani

In my twenties, I was a terribly vivacious girl. A tell-it-like-it-is cheerleader with a "can do" attitude. It wasn't cocky arrogance; it was a comfort in my own skin. That special blend of confidence and sass that youth stitches together so effortlessly. Looking back, it was an awesome state of mind. And it afforded me many friends because that kind of energy is contagious. Because they loved the way I believed in myself, and they loved the way I believed in them. They wanted to feel it too!

I was lighthearted in decisions because roadblocks felt like challenges and failure felt like part of the adventure. I zigged and zagged, and I had a lot fun doing it. I was Albert Einstein in a blonde ponytail, without fear of failure and no need for perfection because perfection wasn't the goal. Inventing myself was. You get this, right? That whole "the world is your oyster" song and dance?

I had two bachelor's degrees and was trying to decide on a master's degree. From a small town in Pennsylvania, I moved to

Arizona. With their tongues in their cheeks, my friends asked, "Are you going there to find yourself?" To which I replied, "I'm going there to *create* myself."

Fast forward a bit down my timeline, and you'll find yourself in my land of dreams come true, complete with a job that feels an awful lot like cheerleading for my favorite team, a Prince Charming of my very own, and two kids who are the lights of my life.

But it hasn't always been this way.

I knew I was going to love motherhood. But I didn't know *I* was going to disappear into that love and practically need a snorkel to breathe. When you love like that, it's easy to get lost in it, and that's where I had some learning to do.

When my children were born, I chose to table my career for a while. I was fortunate to have that choice to begin with, and I made it without hesitation. I loved the idea of teaching them fundamentals and being there for all the firsts. I loved taking the best pieces of myself, attempting to improve my weaknesses, and then diligently packing them away inside their little minds.

The things I had put on hold or filed away in "Maybe Someday" began to smolder, and the embers of my dreams deferred caught fire as she spoke, "Your 'Maybe Someday' is maybe right now."

It's so easy to lose yourself, isn't it? To get buried beneath the duties of motherhood? The daily grind, the never-ending cries for help, the fatigue you fight with your third cup of coffee. You know you haven't always felt so disconnected from . . .*you.*

One fateful morning I opened my eyes and took my first deep breath as a forty-year-old. I was happy! Life felt *right*. But I immediately found myself in a state of reflection. All the things I'd heard about that milestone birthday and swore I'd never have to do—assess my progress, rethink my choices, make new plans, and reconcile my past—I found myself following suit. To my surprise, some things didn't add up. Where was the career? Where was my purpose? Had I fallen short without realizing it? Was I a failure at forty?

I looked in the mirror and searched for some sign of that vivacious twenty-year-old within. Did she just vanish? Abandon me? Give up on me and disappear? I may have even spoken aloud, "Where are you?"

I became acutely aware of a change in the landscape that must have quietly transpired as it was drowned out by the noise of raising kids.

It happens when the kids go to school. They can grab their own snacks. They can tie their own shoes. Their world is expanding along with their curiosity and desire to go it alone.

Suddenly, you find yourself in an empty living room and the silence screams at you.

"Well, what now?"

Do you know what happens in empty spaces?

Something as soft as a whisper *echoes*.

You recognize that voice. It's her. That girl. "I'm right here! Every time you cheer your kids, that's my voice. All the ambition you nurture in them, that's my spirit. The confidence you inspire in them, that's my essence. I've been behind the scenes the whole time."

Her reconnection sparked the old ideas in me. The things I had put on hold or filed away in "Maybe Someday" began to smolder, and the embers of my dreams deferred caught fire as she spoke, "Your 'Maybe Someday' is maybe right now."

That was my call to action. It was *my turn* to dust off my dreams. I listed my wants and needs. I surveyed my skill set and sought out a career that would tie each of those strands into my life's work. I began to honor that girl who believed in herself and believed in others. Who cheered people on and illuminated their potential. That girl wasn't finished inventing herself—and hopefully never will be.

If you're reading this, and a little place in you aches to awaken that dreamer girl inside, then get yourself a cup of tea and listen to the silence.

It's harder to lose yourself than you think.

"Having children is my greatest achievement. It was my savior. It switched my focus from the outside to the inside. My children are gifts; they remind me of what's important."

—Elle Macpherson

4

I'M BREATHING AND NEVER LEAVING

by Christi McGuire

"I don't want to go home! I'm a terrible mom, aren't I?" I hit send on the text message and pressed my face against the dirty hotel window as tears ran down my cheeks, drawing avenues into the dusty film on the glass.

I closed my eyes and listened to the sound of traffic from the twenty-eighth floor of my hotel. It wasn't the luxurious Marriott rooms we were accustomed to in Florida—spacious and adorned with elaborate swimming pools, ocean views, and drinks with colorful umbrellas. It was a downgraded hotel chain in the middle of Manhattan. A crackerjack box by comparison, but I didn't care. It was beautiful to me.

That night was my sixth and last in New York City, and the thought of leaving it made me delirious with dread. I wanted to stay forever in this ten-by-ten room with the broken TV remote, stiff bath towels, and gummy carpet.

I cried one of those ugly cries, full of all the emotion you only let go when it's too powerful to hold in. All because I didn't want to go home! And then I felt guilty about not wanting to go home! Talk about a temper tantrum—I was having one on the corner of 5th and 40th, across the street from the New York Public Library. I, being an editor, writer, and book lover, had to step away from the biggest, most beautiful library in the biggest, most beautiful city in the country? As if that didn't add insult to injury . . . I mean, come on! Could fate have taunted me anymore?

I wiped my tears and opened my eyes to stare at all the bright lights of that sleepless city, dazzling and showing off outside the small window frame, fueled by the energy and promise and aspirations of all the people who lived there. Worked there. Made their way and built their futures in the one city in the world where making it at all means making it everywhere.

I took a deep breath full of the evening air. Even inside the hotel room I could inhale it because it was New York, and New York air is made up of this magical stuff that permeates walls and windows. I felt like I could breathe for the first time in years. Really breathe, and I didn't want to stop breathing. For nearly an entire week, I'd combined work and pleasure in NYC with one of my best friends— my college roommate from twenty-some years ago—and I had been *breathing.*

We'd gone breathing through the Empire State Building, Grand Central Station, and The Met. We'd breathed our way through Central Park, Rockefeller Center, and three (yes, three!) Broadway shows. We slept in (squeal!). We ate when we wanted to, and I didn't have to cut up anybody's food or share my dessert. We did what we wanted when we wanted and without any consideration for piano lessons, sports practices, and homework. I wasn't drowning in the never-ending to-do lists and the rat race of packing lunches, driving carpool, scheduling playdates, volunteering for Girl Scouts, meal-planning, grocery shopping—all on top of working full time in my small home office in the back of the house where I only leave when I'm leaving for someone else.

I was just *me* in NYC. Even physically I was more free. For those few days, I had no anxiety, depression, migraines, indigestion, whining, or complaints. I was a person with a fully functioning and free body, able to go and do and be and feel.

At some point, I realized it wasn't New York I was afraid to leave behind. It was the fact that I knew I'd be leaving *myself* behind too.

So how was I supposed to leave that spirit of me to wisp through the skyline alone?

I guess part of me expected to feel the freedom of being my own person again for a few days. But there was this thing that caught me off guard. This discovery of something stuffed so far into a corner of my mind I'd have never known was there if the city lights hadn't so fully illuminated it.

For two of the days, I was there for a conference, and I'd walk along the buzzing streets with other professionals, all hurrying to and from their pockets of success on this amazing island in the world where people *make it*. I'd walk to the Graduate Center of the City University of New York, showered and dressed in this cloak of professionalism that I didn't want to trade back in for the sweats I wear in my home office. The one I sit in every day so we have the funds for fun things like going to the movies or to Disney World. So I can be available to my family whenever they need me, instead of being tied to a cubicle from nine to five.

Sometimes, that home office feels like a prison I voluntarily lock myself inside. Maybe it's because, somewhere along the way, it stopped feeling like I volunteered. Somewhere along the way, I forgot I chose this path and that I once enjoyed it. It all became expected; it even felt demanded at times.

And so I didn't want to leave the energy I felt walking along the streets of NYC to sit in my prison cell full of laundry and dirty dishes and real-life demands, simply because my leave was up. I wanted to stay and feel all successful-like with my washed hair and ironed clothes.

And that night, washing the windows with my tears, I realized all of it. That my life—the one I've built out of love and sacrifice—felt like Alcatraz. And I marinated in my own sadness and guilt all evening.

I felt like a horrible mother for even identifying it.

I shouldn't feel like this! I scolded myself. *I should be missing my wonderful husband and kids much more than I have been. Right? Am I an ingrate? Am I selfish? Why aren't I more anxious to leave and get back home?*

About that time, Melissa's text reply buzzed me out of my funk: *You bleed out every other day for everyone else, so I'd say you've earned some time to just be all about you! You don't want to leave, but yet you will. And that's what makes you a great mom.*

I smiled a little and sniffed a little too. *A great mom.* Is that what a great mom is made of? I wasn't so sure. A great mom probably would have been ready to climb through broken glass and rusty nails to get home.

But maybe I was wrong. Maybe that's exactly what a great mom is made of. Maybe the greatest mom version inside of us is the one who doesn't necessarily feel like showing up. The one who doesn't want to give up the last Hershey kiss. Who doesn't want to leave the weekend getaway with her friends. Who doesn't want to get up early and taxi kids around or sit at the ball field for hours on end. Maybe the greatest mom doesn't want to cancel her hair appointment for a field trip or spend her spare cash on new volleyball shoes or give up her Saturdays for travel tournaments.

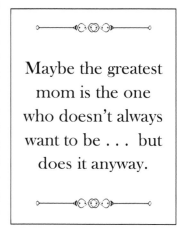

Maybe the greatest mom is the one who doesn't always want to be . . . but does it anyway.

Maybe the greatest mom is the one who doesn't always want to be . . . but does it anyway.

I slowly folded those professional clothes and placed them in the bottom of my suitcase. I promised myself I'd try dressing up more, maybe. Make an effort to get out of the house and the office and all the traps therein. I swore I'd register for more conferences and find more ways to connect with other professionals. I left the city making all sorts of commitments to myself of remedies and consolation prizes. Ones I mostly knew would never come to fruition, but the hope of them gave me the energy to get on the plane, anyway.

And that family of mine? Well, guess who was at the airport, racing around the corner with arms wide and smiles wider, just at the sight of me? I let myself sink into those hugs and smell their precious little girl scent.

Turns out I was still breathing. The air was just different. I listened to them eagerly tell me about their time while I was away. It didn't sound a thing like the hustle and bustle of busy city streets, but it still sounded like energy. And over and over again they hugged me and said how much they missed me. That sometimes unkempt mom in the home office. The one who occasionally feels like she's going nowhere fast and who sometimes feels ashamed over it. The one with tears all over her clothes in the suitcase.

They missed *her*.

And guess what? The absence of those New York city lights lit up something inside me that I was glad to discover.

I missed them too.

TEMPER TANTRUM

I didn't realize when I bought a house with a
mud room that I was opening a Payless shoe store.
Shoes galore thrown on the floor. Not *into* the three
baskets designated for shoes. No, *next to* the baskets
designated for shoes. Not *into*. *Next to*. Three pairs of flip
flops, two pairs of boots (one suede, one leather), four
pairs of sandals, two pairs of sneakers.
And three empty baskets.

5

HERE, TAKE MY SUNSET

by Melissa Rixon

I dropped off my daughter at her Tuesday night orchestra rehearsal and made a beeline for Lido Beach. It's around the corner, and if I hurry, I'm guaranteed nearly two hours of peace and quiet and salty air. Typically, I'm a tired and harried mother. So I protect my Tuesdays like my basset hound protects his milk bones—with lots of snarling and a little bit of drool.

I brought my work with me, which isn't necessarily the stuff of serenity, but writers live and die by deadlines, so my work usually travels where I do. You get what you get and you don't throw a fit and all that. This is what I get.

I kicked off my shoes and started the walk through the cool sand toward the shore. The breeze instantly relaxed me. A good minute passed before I was even aware of the cleanse I was feeling in my chest.

I had fallen into a hypnotic trance, my eyes fixed on the changing sky, the water calling me closer with each gentle lap of a small wave, when . . . "Ouch!" I stepped on a nasty sand spur. I plucked it from my foot, and maybe said something a little naughty while I fought back the urge to be irritated, anxious to get back to the comfort of my hypnosis and revel in the abounding peace.

I set up my scarce office while the sun lazily made its way to the horizon in front of me and a yoga instructor calmly lead a class behind me. It had all the makings of a vacation flyer you'd send to some stressed-out executive freezing his butt off up north. *I might be driven by deadlines, but it beats fluorescent lights and number crunching,* I thought.

In the distance were the squeals of two little girls—sisters I'd guessed—chasing each other up and down the nearly empty beaches until the younger of the two raced up to me to say hi.

"Well, hi." I smiled back. She was about four years old, from what I could guess, and a perfect blend of curious and charming.

"Whatcha read'n?" she asked, fighting the sticky ropes of hair plastered to her cheeks.

"Oh, I'm just working on some things." I wasn't trying to blow her off, exactly, but . . . tick tock. "Have to leave shortly."

"You gonna do that the whole time?" she asked.

I smiled again and lightly giggled. "Well, I have a little girl too, and right now she's at violin practice, and so I'm working while she's there." It was a hint she was happy to ignore.

"What does she look like?" she asked.

"She has blond hair and blue eyes, and she loves the beach. Just like you."

In a blink she was off again. Running back and forth, switching between animal identities while she chased her older sister, growling, hissing, and barking along the way, before she grew bored with it and made her way to me once more.

"Wanna be my baby dinosaur?" she asked. She was the cutest little nuisance.

"Well, I—"

"Here." She took her sandy towels and tossed them into my lap. "You are my baby, and those are your blankets." In the sand she drew an oval around me with her tiny finger. "This is your egg, and you can't leave your egg."

I might as well have brought my own kids, I thought and closed my notebook. I glanced at the mother, who was either completely checked out or simply unfazed by the fact that a stranger was now babysitting her girls. *Don't mind me*, I thought. *It's an even trade. I'll entertain your kids, and you can watch my sunset.*

The little girl flapped her wings and ran around my egg, screeching and aggressively fighting off imaginary predators. "We are pterodactyls!" She flapped her wings. "Just stay right there, and I'll protect you!"

Her mother, still in her chair, turned at the sound of her daughter's hollering, made brief eye contact with me, and then turned back to face the sun.

Yes, your daughter's sandy towels are all over me. Yes, I am here for a few scarce hours of solitude, and they are interrupting my work. But please! Don't get up.

But the truth was that the little girl was delightful, and I enjoyed her bold imagination and lack of inhibition. I laid my notebook aside and sank into the whimsy while she defended me from all the invisible danger closing in.

When she was tired of squawking and fighting off our enemies, she sat down next to me.

"Ya know those stickers?" she asked. "The ones that pinch you?"

"Oh, yes, the sand spurs? I stepped on one coming out here. Be careful running around. They hurt."

"I know. I stepped on one too. But look out there."

I turned and looked in the direction of her gesture.

"See those sticks? There's a sticker under each one. I buried them, so don't step where you see a stick. And if you see a circle in the sand with a line through it, don't step there either. I ran out of sticks, so I just buried them and drew that over it."

I looked out over the beach. There had to be a hundred sticks and even more circles with lines through them.

"You are a very thoughtful little girl," I said. "Thank you for making the beach safe." She puffed up at the praise. "That must have taken you a long time. How long have you been here?"

"Since before I ate my lunch," she said, and with that she was reenergized for another round of pretend. "Now we're the big dinosaurs. The Tonnasaurus Rex." She growled and swatted the air.

"It's Tyrannosaurus Rex." Her old sister approached just in time for a big sisterly correction. "Mom's ready to go."

She happily told me good-bye and ran toward her mother who was packing up her things and looking around for what I assumed were the towels.

I gave them a gentle shake, folded them up, and walked them over.

"Your girls are adorable," I said.

She was tired. I could see that now. Her eyes were set deep in dark circles, and I heard the exhaustion in the emptiness of her voice.

"I hope they didn't get sand all over you," she said.

"Ah, well, you know. It's the beach." I smiled.

She nodded, still wrestling with a far-off gaze, and she walked away.

I sat back down, wrapped my arms around my knees, and watched the sun make its final descent into the watery unknown. When it disappeared, I collected my few things and began the walk back, carefully sidestepping the many sticks and circles placed for the protection of everyone. I stopped for a minute in the twilight and took in the sight once more—the peppering of warnings of a sweet, little Tonnasaurus Rex, and then I said a silent prayer for her very *human* mommy, who'd no doubt modeled what it means to fiercely and diligently protect others, even though she barely had the strength to stand today.

> Maybe there had been too many mom-days in a row without a break.

I thought about her on the way to my car, that mother who no doubt needed me, the stranger, that evening. And for reasons I'll never know. Maybe she was processing terrible news of sickness or death or a runaway husband. Maybe she was making the tough choices left to grown-ups and simply couldn't be a baby dinosaur while she did it. Or maybe there had been too many mom-days in a row without a break.

What I do know is there is much to learn from my encounter with that spirited girl and her dispirited mother—about the importance of looking out for each other. Whether it's sticks and signs drawn in sand to warn strangers on a beach, fierce flapping and screeching to protect what we love, or simply carrying the load of a weary stranger for a couple of hours, giving her the gift of a sunset. There's a space for each of us to make life better for having been there . . . and I hope to know them and do my part, each time I arrive.

THINGS NO ONE TELLS YOU

School supply lists are no longer basic and essential.
Do not be alarmed if you see things like
"passport" and "iPad."

School projects are now called "Family Projects."
This is because your child cannot do them alone. You are
back to having homework. And it's graded harder than
you remember. So try YOUR best.

Flat Stanley is going to happen to you.
You are going to hate Flat Stanley.

Your child will bring home a classroom stuffed animal
named something like "Chomp" or "Mr. Snickers."
It is likely crawling with germs and probably lice,
yet you will be pressured to take it on a weekend vacation
so you can "document" its time with your "fun" and
"exciting" family through photographs you glue into a
classroom journal.

You will probably never print any of the actual photos
you ever take, other than the ones with that classroom
stuffed animal.

6

TAKE TEN

by Teri Mirikitani

I was at the ballfield. Again. For the fourth time in a week. Déjà vu hit me as I climbed the bleachers and saw another tired mom eating a hotdog and staring blankly over the cheering crowds and clouds of clay dust. I could tell she was not okay, because I've had that faraway look before, so I smiled brightly and greeted her with an upbeat hello. She gave me a helpless glance that said *I am about to crack.* So I gently tried to open the door of conversation with her, hoping to lighten her load and brighten her day a bit.

As she slowly nudged the door open, she admitted, with shame in her voice, "Do you know this is the fourth hotdog I've eaten at this ballpark this week?" She proceeded to recount how her day slipped from one chore to the next and how it became such a blur that, after getting her children out the door and on time to their sports, she realized, "I don't even take time to feed myself!"

Being so busy that we forget to take care of ourselves is so common in motherhood that it's nearly epidemic. Not taking the time to feed ourselves is only one of the ways we neglect our well-being. Many moms I talk to admit to not keeping regular doctor appointments, yet they wouldn't think of missing their children's annual check-ups. They wear the same clothes they've owned for eight years, while their kids leave the house in all the current fashion trends. They lament having no time to exercise, while their kids are shuttled from activity to activity every night of the week. Their lives are put on pause, while their children's lives are actively enriched.

If our basic needs aren't being met, then you can imagine where the "extras" might fall on the priority list. The things we'd *like* to do. The things that blow our hair back and make life easier or more exciting.

There are, of course, what I call the gifted master planners. I have such admiration for these women. You know who they are because you receive their Christmas cards the day after Thanksgiving. They can make costumes, feed the homeless, and build award-winning science projects from the things they keep in their purses. And they've run more miles on foot than you've actually driven this month. For those of you who are this type of woman, this may not apply to you. You probably have all of this figured out.

I'm speaking to the mom whose minutes of the day bleed and blur until you lay your head on the pillow at night, feeling like you've accomplished practically nothing at all and certainly nothing for yourself. To you, I'd like to introduce what I call "Take Ten." I've adopted this approach in my own life to get the ball rolling on new ideas, dreams, goals—anything that needs attention but yet gets away from me. All it requires is ten minutes. Who doesn't have ten minutes? It relieves the pressure of trying to find an hour, or even a half hour, to complete a task. I could find the pot of gold at the end of the flippin' rainbow long before I could ever find a half hour with nothing already scheduled in it. If we wait for that kind of time, we'll never begin. And to never begin is a far worse tragedy than never finishing.

As a mom, you likely have a staggering list of tasks and chores to be completed throughout the day. No matter the age of your kiddos, whether toddlers or teenagers, moms are the personal managers and assistants to everyone under the roof. But ten minutes is doable somewhere in the day. And you may be surprised at the many things you can do in that time that will enhance your life.

Look at your already jammed schedule and find only ten minutes. To get you started, here are lists with suggested ways to fill it up.

Work toward your personal professional goals:
- Read some kind of relevant material.
- Make a school admissions counselor appointment.
- Schedule an informational interview with an expert in your field of interest.
- Search job boards.
- Search Pinterest.
- Seek a consultant.
- Write down tools/skills/resources you have.
- Write down tools/skills/resources you need to acquire.
- Write down the steps in which you must proceed.

Work toward self-enrichment:
- Work out (try one of many ten-minute workout apps).
- Learn a new language.
- Meditate. Pray.
- Practice an instrument.
- Read a book, blog, or daily devotional.
- Stretch. Do yoga.
- Call a friend or family member to connect and catch up.
- Do a craft.
- Work toward organization and scheduling (take a moment to untangle all the strings pulling on you, line them up, and devise a plan to knock them out).
- Plan the next day's schedule and review in the evening.
- Plan a healthy meal or snack for the next day or week.

Work on kids' school requirements for the next day:
- Get kids started on homework.
- Sign permission slips.
- Read the school newsletter and update your calendar.
- Lay out uniforms for sports.
- Gather supplies for after-school clubs or projects.

In whatever way you use this approach, it is freewheeling and up to you. However, there is one way to use Take Ten that I consider a must because it contributes to your overall health and well-being. Carve out time to recenter, recharge, and refocus. Same time every day, or take it whenever needed—it's a carry along—but it's mandatory. Be still and give yourself the gift of silence, suppress the incessant chatter in your brain, and let it all go for a few moments. Stop and take in the peace and quiet. Just be you. Breathe. Count. Repeat a loving, positive phrase. If you find it difficult to sit still, do some gentle stretches. This is an amazing combo for relaxation and rejuvenating your body. Do whatever it takes to unplug. The earth will not stop spinning, the sky won't fall, and life will continue. You will feel lighter, more relaxed, and better equipped to handle the rest of the day—as well as your next ten-minute challenge.

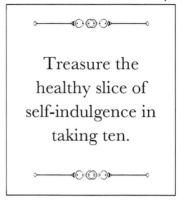

Treasure the healthy slice of self-indulgence in taking ten.

Whatever you'd like to begin new or do better, start giving it ten minutes. You'll be surprised at the magic that can happen with the seemingly small amount of time.

The payback? A spark of happiness and excitement. A rush of satisfaction that you used to feel when you were blazing the trail full of possibility into your young adulthood. You'll feel a sense of accomplishment, a sense of pride in moving toward your own goals, the delight of mental stimulation, and the reward of doing something that is for no one but you!

Most importantly, you will be guilt-free for snagging such a small amount of time. You will treasure that healthy slice of self-indulgence. It may sound over-simplified, but simplicity is almost always a wise investment.

What do you have to lose? Ten minutes? You can afford it. You may just enjoy it, and the reward will whet your appetite for your next ten. Get started!

"I think it's great when women talk about things.
I'm all about female empowerment. There's a lot of
lonely, lost moms out there. Moms need to be encouraged
to tell the truth. There's a lot of glamour mommy stuff.
It's OK to get real."

—Kelly Cutrone

7

SKINNY DIPPING

by Christi McGuire

Get this. I have discovered the cure for anxiety, depression, and all those vile feelings you get when you are over-worked and over-tired. And here's the best part. It's not a pill or a workout program that will sweat you dry; it's free, and it's a miracle. A free miracle. Can you even take it?

Okay, here it is . . .

Skinny dipping. Full Monty, buck naked, birthday suit swimming.

Yes, that's right. Go ahead and read that again. I'll wait. I want you to really let it sink in, because it's crazy and crazy things take a minute.

I discovered this gem one day while working in my home office, where I sit in a straight-backed chair all day long. I walk like a humped-over, old lady—the one from Hansel and Gretel, I think—because I'm slumped at my computer for what seems like a bazillion hours every day. So I was at my desk, staring at the sparkling blue swimming pool just outside my window. It was inviting and impossible to ignore.

I can't. Can I? I shouldn't. Should I? I could. Couldn't I?

My husband was away visiting clients. I had no conference calls. No packages or visitors were expected to show up at my door.

So . . . I could. And I did.

I skipped that whole exhausting, mind-numbing, soul-crushing step of stuffing myself into a spandex, control-top, bathing suit.

I quickly shrugged off my clothes, wrapped a bath towel around myself, and tip-toed out to the patio. I was like a naughty teenager sneaking out in the middle of the night, only I was a naked forty-year-old in broad daylight.

I put a toe in the water, and a sly smile crept across my face in satisfaction. The Florida sunshine had simmered the water to perfection. I looked around foolishly, as if waiting for the paparazzi to start leaping out of the bushes with cameras. But there wasn't a peep. Not a sound. Not the soft rustle of a leaf or the scampering of a squirrel. Nothing. I dropped the towel and charged into the pool.

Wow. Wow. Wow! Was this awesome! As soon as my shoulders slipped under the water, my troubles melted away, along with the anxiety about my workload and the to-do list scrolling out of control in my life.

I giggled a little. I went under. I slipped in and out of the surface like a happy goldfish. I floated on my back for a while and stared at the blue skies above. I swam laps back and forth and imagined I was Michael Phelps (but with baby bulge and C-section scars).

I was free and ridiculous and breaking all the rules. And just as I was beginning to feel the shock over the potential lapse in my own judgement, I got distracted by something so amazing that I audibly exclaimed, "Oh, my, YES!"

Do you know what? Do you *even* know what?

Boobs float in water. (Good Lord, I hope my pastor never reads this.)

My boobs were buoyant. Floating. Like life preservers. Like happy, bouncy, sunny, carefree, and doctor-manipulated boobs, they were at attention.

Well, I should just stay here forever, I thought. In the crystal blue water, the sun on my shoulders, with my gravity-defying boobs.

But as it tends to do, duty called. I sneakily surveyed the yard and exited the pool, greeted gravity with a grunt of disapproval, and wrapped myself back in my towel. I dried off the water—and my sexiness with it—and then made the slow-going journey back to reality, where I came to a happy realization.

I didn't feel anxious. I wasn't freaking out about all the things I should have done during those twenty minutes in my birthday suit. I didn't feel that tightness creeping in around my shoulders and up my neck.

> I was like a naughty teenager sneaking out in the middle of the night, only I was a naked forty-year-old in broad daylight.

Instead, I felt free from all the demands I tend to impose on myself, as if they'd been stripped away with my Capri pants and T-shirt.

I showered, did my hair and makeup, and folded myself back inside my constricting clothes. All the evidence of a woman walking on the wild side disappeared. Only the slightly mischievous smile remained fixed on my face the rest of the day.

I was happy, calm, and content, all the way into the witching hour while I brewed up dinner, chased kids into beds, and began preparations for the next day. I was light and cheery and hard to frustrate. I wasn't wallowing in the unchecked items of things to do; I was reveling in the freedom from it.

And that feeling bled into the next day and then the next as I took my daily dip.

The change in my attitude begged my husband to ask, "Things are going well?"

"Guess what I did," I whispered. "I went skinny dipping the other day, and I loved it so much that I did it again. I might even do it again today. Wanna come?"

He laughed, obviously a bit impressed with my out-of-character adventure, and then quickly warned me to avoid Wednesdays. "Pool service," he reminded me with a wink.

"Oh, no . . . wouldn't want to tempt the pool boy," I teased.

So here's the take away. I didn't tell you this story so you'd go swim naked in your backyard. For one, I live in the country with no neighbors. Nobody can see me except for the buzzards, squirrels, and salamanders that scurry around the yard. If you live in a neighborhood, this could go very badly for you, and I'm not sure I can afford to bail a bunch of naked ladies out of jail.

But skinny dip. Not in the literal sense—in the metaphorical sense. Find a way to strip down to your bare needs. Shrug off the confines of to-do lists and schedules and all the anxiety that comes with them. Take the plunge into the cool waters of something just for you. Wiggle around in the refreshing pool of freedom for a few minutes here and there. Play a game on your phone. Have a piece of chocolate and dance in your living room. Read a book. (Read *this* book.) Do something ridiculous.

Give yourself the gift of a fresh breath. Your to-do list won't ignite into flames. Your schedule won't erupt like Mount St. Helens. Dinner will still get cooked, and kids will still get shuttled to soccer. But taking that breath—that daily skinny dip—will reignite you. Let that energy run and seep into those parts of your days that feel like more of the same.

Turn routine upside down and go get naked.

CHRISTI'S MOTHERHOOD RESUME

Look what I can do . . .

- Cut up waffles into equal sized, buttered and syrup-ed pieces.
- Pony tails. I can pull thin, fine, pin-straight hair into a ponytail, in the dark with one hand tied behind my back.
- Push in dining room chairs (this is a big deal because I am the only one in my family who knows how to do this).
- Get stains out of clothes (one day I will write an entire book on this subject).
- Refill the butter dish so it is softened in time for the above-mentioned waffles.
- Replace the toilet paper rolls. In all three bathrooms.
- Refill soap dispensers.
- Make Crock-Pot® dinners that everyone hates.
- Create, order, stamp, address, and mail Christmas cards. Just in time for New Year's Eve.
- Replace batteries and buy batteries in bulk and remember which thing needs which, what, and how many batteries. I'm just really good at batteries.
- Keep everybody's favorite condiment in the refrigerator lest they won't eat their Crock-Pot® chicken.
- Store a miniature Office Depot in my closet.
- Make PB and J (it's all about the ratios, people).
- Keep paper in the printer, tissue boxes replenished, and snacks in the pantry.
- Schedule . . . *Everything.*
- Make "homemade" pancakes with Bisquick.
- Iron the 372 Girl Scout Patches my girls earned (or beg Grandma to do it).
- Keep track of the 924 passwords required to access our electronic lives.
- Take pictures but never organize them.
- Disinfect. Because children are carrier monkeys.
- Quiz spelling words, math facts, vocabulary words, and state capitols while I make snacks, breakfast, lunch, and dinner.

TEMPER TANTRUM

Recorder Concert: Sixty or so third-graders blowing
heavily into cheap flutes does not a concert make.
Headaches? Yeah, they make those.

8

INVISIBLE DAVE

by Melissa Rixon

Let me begin by saying I was a teeny tiny, little bit stressed out. For starters, the elementary school had scheduled every field trip, field day, awards ceremony, poetry reading, class party, and teacher conference into the space of one week. I had a migraine. My husband was out of town. And every time I opened an e-mail or answered the phone, someone was on the other end needing party supplies, extra sunscreen, a chaperone, more pencils, a ride, or a favor. All the needs I was so used to meeting and all the balls I was so accustomed to juggling suddenly grew thorns and bad attitudes.

I just wanted to quit. At everything.

I wasn't sick of people needing me. I wasn't feeling like they were taking advantage. But I was up against another self-imposed deadline . . . the thirty-fifth one, I think. And, yet again, the deadline was near and my novel was nowhere near finished. Instead, it sat glowing on my laptop screen while I made another trip to the grocery store to buy string cheese for first graders.

You see, over time, I've learned to divide each day in two parts:

Part One: Kids at School

Part Two: Kids at Home

It's during Part One that I must tend to my professional goals and aspirations. It's also during Part One that I grocery shop, clean my house, get my hair done, take care of personal correspondence, work out, pay the bills, and fold laundry. It's during Part One that I make a *home* and I make *me*. Part Two is for living in the home I make and melting into the landscape of it. And while that's okay, it mostly means I keep pushing back personal goals because there isn't enough real estate in Part One for making *deadlines*.

On this particular day, I'd come home from chaperoning first-grade field-day sack races, and with approximately two hours left in Part One of the day, the phone rang. I took a deep breath and listened to it ring again. And again. Each time, I meant to answer it, but I was unable to wrestle myself into the act of picking up the line. Before I ever got around to it, the answering machine picked up instead. (Yes, we still have an answering machine. It's because we're so high-tech. Like the Jetsons.)

My ears perked up while I strained to hear the voice in the speaker as I sank into my couch and stared at the ceiling. It was one of those super long messages that get annoying because they're too informative and seem to never end.

"Um, yes. Hi, Mrs. Rixon, this is Dave with the early childhood center, and I've been trying to reach you for over a week now. I need to conduct the final interview regarding your son Michael. This will conclude the longitudinal study we started six years ago. We appreciate your continued cooperation, as this study has given us a lot of information that should help us improve our educational standards and identify correlations between home and school, but we really need to wrap it up. I will be at his school next week and would like to have the final interview completed before then."

Now, mind you, Dave was not at fault here. I fully acknowledge that. Dave was doing his job. Dave needed to ask me questions. I'd agreed to this study when my oldest son was in kindergarten because it was meant to be low-key and not time-consuming at all. It provided information to the Department of Education about how differently children perform in school based on their home lives. It was great, and I was all in, but on that Friday morning, I didn't want to hear that Dave had a file he needed to close out. That *Dave* had needs. At that moment, with my unfinished book still blinking in the backdrop of my life, Dave became the embodiment of every reason that book was unfinished. Frustration broke me. One of those cry-lumps jammed in my throat, and my eyes got hot. Everything around me started to slide sideways as I shouted into my empty living room, "Yeah, well, get in line, Dave!"

I stomped across the room. "Of course you need something from me DAVE. You and everyone else! You barely even KNOW me, but you've already gotten the memo, haven't you? Melissa Rixon doesn't have a life! Melissa Rixon has no ambition or dreams or desires of her own. She just wants to make your world go 'round, doesn't she, Dave?" I picked things up and slammed them back down. My dog hid in the corner of my bedroom.

> All those needs I was so used to meeting and all the balls I was so accustomed to juggling suddenly grew thorns and bad attitudes.

Oh, I was completely and fully aware of how irrational I sounded. I just didn't friggin' care anymore. I grabbed my purse and stormed out of the house and, with my dander up, drove straight to Target to buy a green shirt my daughter needed to wear to the field trip at the planetarium and the detergent I needed to wash the baseball playoff uniform. All the way there I shouted at poor, unsuspecting Invisible Dave.

"Ya know, Dave. I have dreams. I have goals. I have ideas, and I'm smart. And yet, I've spent the past eleven years of my life spinning my wheels into the muck. Do you even know what that feels like, Dave? Of course not. I'll bet you're living the dream interviewing tired moms every day, aren't you, Dave? At the very least, you're doing something for YOU."

My tires squealed a little as I turned into the parking lot. It sounded like rebellion in those tires, and I liked it. I liked the way it felt to throw my minivan around that way. I was driving up and down the parking lot, simultaneously irritated with the fact the place was so crowded and also sympathetic because of course it was. It was full of moms tending to Part One of the day. And time was running out because Part Two was closing in! We were about to turn into pumpkins. I circled again and again until I screeched into a spot, walked inside.

And there. *There.* Right in front of me dressed head-to-toe in a Buzz Lightyear costume was a little boy about two years old. A shaggy, blonde mop of hair flopping over his eyes. He was pressing all the fake buttons on his sleeve and making laser noises with his mouth. Without wanting to—and without even a warning—I started to cry so hard I ushered myself back out to that rebellious minivan and sobbed all over my steering wheel.

You see, my great, big first-grader used to love to wear his Buzz Lightyear costume to Target. A shaggy mop of blonde hair flopping over his eyes too. And he'd press the buttons and make the noises with his mouth. Yet, just that morning, he'd hopped all over the field outside in a sack race against his big first-grade friends.

In that moment, a little clarity settled in me. Time is moving so fast. I know this. I see it every day in kids painted over in bigger-sized shoes and loose teeth. And how much of it do I spend feeling resentful? That's a shameful thing to admit, right? That sometimes you just want to fast forward to bedtime and skip the whole part of the day where you make the world go around?

But what would happen if you did?

Well, for starters, maybe first-graders wouldn't get their string cheese. Maybe you wouldn't get to play chaperone and sit next to your little girl in her green shirt at the planetarium while she snuggles into your side, so proud that you're there. Maybe you won't get to experience the humming electricity of play-off games. No matter how long they seem to last, there's still a crackling energy there, and you owe it to yourself and your kids to go sit in it.

And maybe . . . just maybe . . . the guy who's diligently collected his data for six years can't close out his file and deserves for you to take the time to call him back.

I picked up the phone and called Invisible Dave and spent the next thirty minutes answering questions about our family life.

Yes, we still eat dinner around the table. Yes, we go to church on Sundays. Yes, we are involved in after-school sports. Yes, we limit screen time. Yes, we read. every day. Yes, we spend quality time together as a family. Yes, we do all of that every day of every week. And yes, my son is a successful student.

For six years his grades have reflected the answers I've given in an interview I rarely feel like giving. But the interview reflects our life. Our home. The stuff I make happen in Part One and Part Two of the day.

It's hard work. It's draining work. Sometimes, it means every one of my personal goals completely stands still. But in the blink of an eye, this devastating things happens. Buzz Lightyear grows up. And that's something we don't want to miss just because we're hoping to expand Part One of the day, obsessed with looming deadlines.

We are the ball jugglers, list makers, and errand runners. We're the house cleaners and dinner makers and laundry washers and classroom helpers. That's who we are right now. But we are something else too. We are the *need meeters*. The mighty *world spinners*. And if deadlines get shuffled around and pushed back—who better to make the adjustments than someone *who can spin the world?*

I still have my freak-out days. The ones where I feel consumed with everyone else's wildfires. The ones where Invisible Dave might want to lie low. I still have my moments when I want to fast forward to bedtime. But that little Buzz Lightyear at Target was a great reminder to keep it all in perspective. To stop rushing and wishing my busyness away.

Because childhood doesn't last to infinity . . . and beyond.

THINGS NO ONE TELLS YOU

Kids' dental needs will take you to the poor house, show you around, and dump you there forever.

Video game music will give you a seizure.

Grocery shopping without kids: $152.37.

Grocery shopping with kids: $879.84.

You will buy every professional photo ever taken of your child, and then you will rent a warehouse in which to store them.

If variety is important to you, you will need to come up with seventeen ways to serve noodles and chicken nuggets.

You will never, NEVER, sleep soundly again.

You will earn an MD by googling symptoms.

The contents of your purse could save the world.

9

LOVE THE BODY

by Teri Mirikitani

Once upon a time, there was a skinnier and younger me. That younger me was tiny and toned, and all my body parts sat exactly where they should, and it was amazing. Ironically, it still was never good enough. I struggled with what every woman seems to struggle with. That catty, inner-bitch who, with disapproving eyes and pursed lips, looks in the mirror, overlooks everything right, and sizes up everything wrong.

Then came my thirties and pregnancies. It's mind-blowing as your body morphs into a Happy Buddha. Everything grows. *Everything.* Things shift to make room for all that growing. Before long, you accidentally see a shadow of yourself, and you begin looking around for the Macy's parade balloon that must be nearby. Then realization hits, and you mutter, "Oh, that's . . . *me.*"

Then come the forties. That's where worlds collide. You hear words like *cottage cheese*, *muffin top*, *saddle bags*, and *arm flap*. Maybe you experience a little jowl action and the tiniest hint of another chin moving in. It's all so confusing because, while our bodies are busy sliding off our bones, nothing will zip you up in the emotional and mental comfort that happens in your forties. Suddenly, there's this confidence in you. This assuredness that you've lived long enough to have a little wisdom, a touch of swagger, and a bit of sass. We feel great. But this evil irony exists on our exterior. Our skin is loosening, and gravity is wrestling it to the floor. We are *aging*.

Oh, these poor bodies. We run them, walk them, stuff brownies into them, and grow babies with them, and they do their best to comply with all we ask of them.

Under-appreciated in our youth, brought to the brink during pregnancy, and downright tired, we look at our bodies and scold, "Do better! Be better! Look better! Change this! Eat that!" All the while we chuck our pennies in the savings jar for trainers and surgeons and skin-care products and exclusive trips to the Fountain of Youth.

Once, I came across an old photo. I remembered the day it had been taken so clearly, and I remembered hating it. *I look fat in this,* I had thought. *I hate the way I'm smiling.* Yet, compared to anything recent, I'd have given anything to look like that again. I sighed with a bit of melancholy, taking stock of my extra fluff and changing face, and then hurried off to the kids' school where I ran into my friend Lora.

"You doin' okay?" she asked. "You look tired."

I was tired. Tired of looking tired.

"Yeah, I'm okay," I sighed. Another conversation turned to the misfortune of getting older. "I'm just trying to get a hold of my mind. It's like, I know I'm getting older, and my body is going to get older too. I try to eat well and exercise, but I'm really struggling with accepting it! Why are we so hard on ourselves?"

The conversation went back and forth for a while about the abusive self-talk in which we, as women, so often engage.

"Ya know, I was dealing with this not long ago," Lora said. "I was complaining to my mom, and she finally said, 'Why are you so hard on yourself? You're beautiful! And face it. You'll look better today than you will tomorrow, so you'd better enjoy it now!' "

I love this pearl of wisdom that Lora's sweet mom shared. Yes! If not now, then when? It was a lightbulb moment. I'm far from perfect, but from that point on I was determined to try harder.

Not to be young, but to be okay with the me who was once young and now is getting older. I decided to start loving my body the way I love other things in my life. To look for the positive things. To nourish and nurture it.

When women come to me and complain about how they look or feel, I respond simply and succinctly . . . *The more you love your body, the more it loves you back.* We have to get away from hating it for what it does or doesn't look like and start loving it for what it *has done* and is doing.

We are programmed to believe that a woman's aging body renders us unproductive, unattractive, and insignificant to society. If we continue to expect it to perform as it did in our youth, then we're destined to feel lacking. We must learn to love it for what it can do now: care for our loved ones, carry us from place to place, allow us to explore new places and experience new things. Just because we aren't shiny and new doesn't mean we are useless. It may just mean we have to tweak a thing or two.

One of the most common complaints I hear is, "I don't feel like myself anymore." If you ever feel like that, then you should know you are not alone. I feel like that from time to time as well. And here is what I know. YOUth is not YOU.

One way to deal with that feeling when it hits you is to Take Ten. Take ten minutes to . . .

- Try a new makeup or hairstyle that gives you a fresh feeling.
- Do research on your changing shape and the fashion trends that will best flatter it.
- Modify your exercise routine to include a few things you enjoy or something new that breaks up your old routine.
- Make a new playlist so you can jam to updated tunes while you work out.
- Find a new, delicious, healthy breakfast that will jump-start your metabolism.
- Start an accountability group of ladies to check in with regarding your personal goals, and check in with them regularly.
- Stretch and hydrate.

We may have lacked the understanding that our bodies would change so much so fast, but that doesn't mean we must lock ourselves up like crypt keepers or strive for the unattainable yesterday. Self-worth and self-acceptance is beautiful. It's a class act that never goes out of style.

We need to stop *belittling* our bodies and start *building* them. *Fortifying* them. *Appreciating* them. Our inner dialogue needs to transition from beating down our bodies to thanking them for all they've done. Begin caring for your body. Treat it with respect and revere it for its accomplishments. Our focus needs to shift from polishing and correcting imperfections to strengthening our bodies, nourishing them, and giving them what they need for quality longevity.

After all, our sisters in their fifties and sixties are standing over there, with wagging fingers and loving warnings, telling us to get ready because menopause is coming, and it only gets harder from there!

Unrealistic expectations will leave us frustrated. So let our minds, bodies, hearts, and spirits powwow *now* and decide ahead of time how we will allow this ever-changing, ever-aging process to affect our happiness.

Let us heed the advice of my sweet friend Lora's mother and "Enjoy it now!" Enjoy it always. Celebrate your body. Love your body.

And it will love you back.

"The natural state of motherhood is unselfishness. When you become a mother, you are no longer the center of your own universe. You relinquish that position to your children."

—Jessica Lange

10

THE PEACOCK IN THE CHICKEN COOP

by Christi McGuire

"Look what showed up today." I read my husband's text message and smiled at the attached picture. A peacock had somehow migrated to our little farm and was already strutting his stuff around the yard like a king, his feathers on display for the peasants to behold. And, oh, were the peasants beholding . . . the goats, the chickens, and the dog would sneak in for a closer look and then scurry out of the way as his enormous tail would bully its way through the increasingly crowded barnyard.

I opened the windows and watched him in the mornings, always on patrol, always showing off. I took dozens of pictures because I loved the way the light picked up the metallic hues of his plumes. I drank my coffee and gazed at this big, beautiful visitor and giggled at the way he seemed to make himself at home. In some ways, I felt like a little girl again.

My grandfather had raised peacocks, and my sisters and I used to run in the open breezes, snatching up the molted feathers and putting them away for safekeeping. It felt nostalgic now, having this bird and watching my own daughters tuck his feathers away to marvel at later.

I was happy. Old McGuire's farm was abuzz with the clucking of chickens, the frolicking of jolly goats, and now the honking of a proud peacock. E-I-E-I-O.

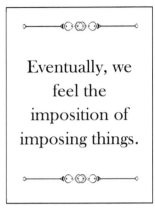

Eventually, we feel the imposition of imposing things.

But as the days unfolded, the now-named Peaty the Peacock became more and more demanding. He needed the most space, he ate all the food, and his once endearing honking became an incessant shrill hollering that interrupted my work and kept me on edge.

One morning, I slipped into my rubber boots and made my way to the barn just in time to see Peaty, imposing as ever, pecking at a chicken. I hurriedly shooed him away and, upon close inspection, realized that many of the chickens had peck marks!

All twenty of our hens were trying to go about their business and dutifully lay their eggs, all while they were being chased, harassed, traumatized, and abused by this consuming and obnoxious, albeit gorgeous, bird.

As much as we enjoyed seeing the peacock, our farm could not sustain him, so we weren't too distraught when he decided to fly away one day and make himself at home at another farm. I miss the ornamentalism. I miss the feathers. But I don't miss his troublesome nature at all.

Do you have a peacock in your chicken coop?

It's a question I'm learning to ask myself about so many things. Are there ornamental things in your life that peck away at the quality of it? I've had friends who've downsized their homes because the upkeep and financial demands were tearing their families apart. I've known people who are being crushed under the weight of debt while they do their best to support cars they can't really afford or send their kids to expensive schools where the cost of kindergarten tuition exceeds any reputable state college.

Maybe it's not financial at all. Maybe you're time poor. You have no time to sit around the kitchen table and swap stories from the day because there are sports or lessons or fitness classes or rehearsals eating away at every spare minute. As a result, you can't remember the last time your whole family just sat and laughed together.

Maybe it's your health. Maybe it's a job. Maybe it's trying too hard to please others or trying to be all things to all people. Maybe it's a desperate sense of purpose or self-doubt or something lacking in a marriage.

Here is what I know: These things can feel like they just show up. At first, it all seems like something to be proud of and admire from your kitchen window. Show off to your friends. Brag about at the office. But, eventually, we feel the imposition of imposing things.

Peaty wasn't a predator or a criminal or a bad guy. He was simply too much for us and the mission of our farm. Now he is doing perfectly well on a property much better suited for him. We can learn something from the reality that exists in that metaphor.

Let me encourage you to be honest with yourself. If you're feeling stressed a little too often, or live camped out on a knife's edge, take some time to take stock of things. Evaluate and reevaluate again and again and again and then fearlessly remove the things that peck away at your mission, your family, your time . . . at *you.*

You will never regret shielding your modest chicken coop from the bold demands of a peacock better suited for another family or another place.

TEMPER TANTRUM

Homework.

Because I love showing the fifth-grade teacher

that I totally get long division.

11

MAKING RAINBOWS

by Melissa Rixon

For the fifth time in a month, I found a clinic slip in my son's backpack.

"Michael, why do you keep going to the clinic for a tummy ache?" I asked. "Is your tummy really hurting or are you making it up?"

"No, it really hurts!" his voice shook when he said it. It was very emotional, this tummy ache.

"Well, then, maybe I need to call the doctor," I said. "It's not normal for you to hurt all the time."

He looked alarmed at the thought of going to the doctor and started to explain a little further. "Well, it doesn't hurt like that. I don't feel sick. I just . . . I just go there because I can lie down for a minute and get some peace and quiet."

Oh, this child. This flesh of my flesh. Five years old and needing fifteen minutes to get away from it all. I batted away images of him in a bubble bath with a chilled eye mask on his face.

I sat down next to him and pulled his legs into my lap. "What is it you feel you need to escape? Let's start with that. Don't you like kindergarten?"

"Mommy, I like it, but I just feel so . . . so wobbly inside! It's almost like every day I go there, and I don't know what's about to happen, and sometimes the kids in my class are nice, and sometimes they say mean things, and sometimes I understand what the teacher is saying, and sometimes I don't, and I just miss being home with you and drinking chocolate milk and eating chicken noodle soup and watching Mickey Mouse. *I miss our house smell.*"

He was homesick. I remember that ache living inside my own wobbly kindergarten tummy all those years ago. When I too would go to the clinic and lie down on the vinyl bed, praying they wouldn't take my temperature—only my word for it—and call my mom. I have that feeling now, from time to time, when I think back on growing up in my old bedroom, listening to mom's beef tips rattle in the pressure cooker while dad watched his westerns on the couch.

And I feel it now. Not for a place, but a time. For way back when Michael seemed too small to walk into a big school by himself with a backpack full of homework and a lunch he'd eat without me.

Truth is, I missed him being home as much as he did. The first day I marched him into that school and set him loose was a day that still hangs cold in my memory. That imposed and mandated division of a mother and her child, at a time neither feel ready, is perhaps one of the most wrenching, yet necessary, milestones of all of life's journeys. Would any child ever go to school if they weren't required? Would they ever be old enough?

I took his hand and closed my eyes. "I want you to imagine something with me, Michael," I said. He followed my lead and closed his eyes tight and wrinkly. "I want you to imagine millions and millions and millions of tiny beads."

"Okay," he said.

"And then I want you to imagine something bumping into them and bending and bouncing off and going this way and that way."

He nodded, and I could almost see his imagination grab its paintbrush, painting pictures in his mind.

"Do you think that might sound like how you feel inside?" I asked.

"Yes," he said. He was serious. So serious, in fact, I had to choke back a giggle in my throat. "It feels like a lot like that. And sometimes it makes my tummy hurt."

"Well, do you know what else feels like that?"

"What?"

"A rainbow. A rainbow is made up of millions and millions of drops of water. More millions than anyone can count. And when sunshine bumps into those water drops, it bends and bounces right off. And while, to me, that sounds like a whole lot of craziness moving around up there in the sky, what I see from down here on earth doesn't look crazy at all. It looks like a pretty piece of art work God hangs up for a while."

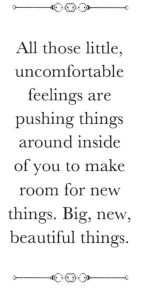

All those little, uncomfortable feelings are pushing things around inside of you to make room for new things. Big, new, beautiful things.

He looked straight ahead, his gears turning and twisting and trying to understand. These poor kids and their metaphor-loving mother.

"You think rainbows are in my belly?" he asked.

"Not exactly, but sort of." I struggled to make it clear. "I'm telling you that all of those bendy, bouncy, wobbly feelings you have are creating something special inside you. You have to feel that way from time to time before you grow up a little more or before you learn something that makes you say 'Wow!' or before you meet a new friend who might still be your friend when you're a grown-up like me. All those little, uncomfortable feelings are pushing things around inside of you to make room for new things. Big, new, beautiful things."

He looked up at the ceiling, and I looked around the room, hoping this weird illustration made as much sense out loud as it did in my head.

"So I need to be happy when I feel like that?"

I kissed the top of head and took in a whiff of his little boy smell. "Don't be afraid of it. You need to recognize it when it shows up. So you can say, 'Oh! This is that feeling I get when I need to think a little harder or ask an important question or be a little bit brave.' "

We were quiet for a few moments before he split the silence with a question.

"Mommy, do you still get that feeling? Even as a grown-up?"

"I still get that feeling every day, Michael. Every single day."

⸺◦◦◦⸺

Michael started middle school a couple of months ago. I spent the entire summer beforehand talking myself into and out of panic attacks. I could hardly sleep the night before, and I wanted to throw up the whole first day. In truth, I wanted to grab him and run away or postpone it all and take a last-minute vacation. Or do something way outside my wheelhouse like homeschool. Anything but subject him to the gauntlet that is a middle-school hallway.

But here we are again, taking on uncertainties one day at a time, and sometimes it feels like thunderstorms, tornados, and hurricanes are pushing their way around inside us now. But we continue that trend of slowly letting go one finger at a time, trusting that even the biggest storms can leave behind a rainbow. And what an unexpected treasure that's become. What promise it holds. Promise of change and unfolding, marching on and growing up, things to come and journeys to travel. Some together and some alone. The promise of color and beautiful light.

THINGS NO ONE TELLS YOU

Your motherly instincts will be so impressively accurate that you may begin to wonder if you're actually psychic.

When your child excels at something, Facebook. Has. To. Know. If Facebook doesn't know, it didn't happen.

The Mama Bear Morph is legit.
Only it's more like Mama Rabid Dinosaur/Tasmanian Devil Hybrid Morph.

If you like clean and tidy, it's best to just turn in your kids or your expectations. The two cannot coexist.

When your child is hungry, he is starving. When your child is thirsty, he is dying. When your child's feet hurt, he needs a wheelchair. There is no such thing as chill.

Babysitters, although worth it, charge a salary, holiday bonuses, a health-care plan, and then go away to college.

A night out begins with a lot of plans and aspirations. It ends at 9:30 with a lot of yawning and eventual snoring.

12

SKIP OF THE DAY

by Teri Mirikitani

One of my favorite memories of my son as a toddler was his skip. From the moment he learned how, he skipped everywhere. He was proud of accomplishing the skip, as are most kids, but Nolan *transformed* the skip. The contentment on his face and the joy while he did it were tangible and made me happy just to watch. Nolan made skipping an art form, and he had many variations, depending on his mood. He pushed the skip to new levels. The width, length, speed, and height would vary. And, for certain, the arms would vary. It was hard to feel grumpy when that little boy skipped.

I remember visiting my family in Pennsylvania one summer when Nolan was about four years old and was skipping around the lake, taking in the amazing buzz of summertime. He was among his grandparents, uncle, aunts, and cousins, having a blast running around a fresh, mountain-spring lake, floating lazily on tubes, and watching family and friends fly down the zip line suspended across the lake and drop into the cool water below. Depending on where they let go determined the height of their free falls, and Nolan was amazed at the bravery he witnessed.

I was sitting under the lakeside pavilion with some family members as we watched the kids running around, enjoying the memories they were making, when someone remarked how nice the scenery was, followed by, "And there's Nolan prancing around the lake!"

I laughed and said, "Actually, he is skipping, not prancing. He skips everywhere, every day. And you know what they say about kids who skip?"

My father, a man of few words, looked up from his chair and directly into my eyes and said, "They're happy."

I smiled and held his gaze and agreed, "Yes, they are."

Sometime later, my younger brother and I were watching Nolan skip, and we agreed how happy it seemed to make him. It looked like freedom, a little escape of anything serious. My brother, Glenn, always the adventurous one and always up for something silly, started skipping with Nolan. Nolan was beyond thrilled—he was doing his favorite thing with his fun-loving uncle.

> We lose the bounce in our step when we are weighed down with doing life as an adult.

And so began their special tradition. They called it the "Skip of the Day." Nolan loved to ask, "Uncle Glenn, did you do your skip for the day?" My brother varied his answers: "Why, yes, I did, Nolan! Thank you!" or "No, I didn't. Let's skip, Cowboy!"

Getting to skip with Uncle Glenn was one of the best parts of Nolan's day. They shared a connection of a carefree moment.

That was such a special memory for me. I loved seeing my son and brother happy together!

What started as fun became an amazing discovery. It was a WOW moment. I had always joined in the skipping and, sure, it was fun. But my brother had given me a new appreciation for it. I realized it wasn't only something that a child could use for fun, but it was also something parents could do with children to jolt them out of a funk, enhance their day, or get them to not be so serious. How can you frown or be angry or serious when you're skipping? Don't believe me? I dare you to try it. Take a skip!

We lose the bounce in our step when we are weighed down with doing life as an adult. But our children give us one of the most beautiful gifts. Being parents lets us relive childhood. We get to experience it through their eyes. We share in it together—all the milestones, discoveries, adventures, traditions, fears, challenges, and successes. Truly, if we step back and see the awesomeness of this opportunity, we can enjoy the beauty this brings to our lives. Adult life is a string of responsibilities, day in and day out. It's easy to lose our lightheartedness. It's easy to forget how to skip.

Not a skipper? Fine. Find something childish and silly. Something that may make you feel momentarily embarrassed if someone were to witness it. This is the beauty of childhood! That carefree and imaginative field where anything is possible. Kids have that magic— the magic we have stifled or buried because we felt that was expected of us as adults. It allows kids to snap out of a mood and into something better.

Let's tap into that magic. Take a moment to talk to a sibling or childhood friend and reminisce about the silly rituals you had. Remember what *your* Skip of the Day was. If you need help, just sit quietly and watch children at a playground. It's an untapped source of ideas.

Everyone has something that lights them up. Rediscover yours and go do it.

"Especially as a woman, your identity changes.
You are now a mom, sort of the most important job
in the world, and the pressure and the guilt and all the
things that are sort of wrapped up in that, I don't think
anyone can prepare you for."

—Anna Faris

13

TRIBES AND TEQUILA

by Christi McGuire

I was working late one night, preparing for the next day—a big day! The launch of a new business!—when I received a message that a lady very dear to me was headed to surgery. "You need to pray. And pray hard. It doesn't look good."

Other than my own mom, Sharon was the number one influence in my life. As my youth group leader, she mothered me through those crazy, tumultuous, teen years. She would gently guide me with her sound advice and loving heart. She was "mama" to many of us. So many kids treading water in the deep of adolescence clung to Sharon, the lighthouse, lifeboat, and lifeline we needed when our own parents seemed out of reach.

That night, as she prepped for surgery many states away, I argued with God. He was preparing my heart to say goodbye, but I simply didn't want to. I pleaded with Him not to take her. I struggled and fought. But I didn't win. She won. Released from the pain and suffering of her human body, she was able to dance through the gates of heaven.

I wanted to rejoice in her eternal homecoming, but I couldn't. A world without her in it seemed . . . wrong.

I bawled all night long until sleep briefly came at four in the morning.

When I awoke, I looked like I'd fought and lost a UFC fight. My makeup was smeared all over my cheeks; my eyes were but tiny slits peeking through the swollen curves of my unrecognizable face. All of it crowned by the sweaty nest of hair styled by my fitful four hours of sleep.

I tried to work, but my heart wasn't in it. I didn't feel like celebrating or basking in any sense of accomplishment. I felt like crawling back into bed and praying it was all a bad dream. I was about to do exactly that when Melissa, unaware of my recent loss and current situation, texted:

We need to get together! I have tons of ideas. I need you to get here and catch them and do that thing you do where you make stuff out of nothing!

But I'm still in my PJs, I weakly typed back.

Who cares! Teri's coming too. Come in whatever you have on! You know we don't care.

Do you have tequila? I joked. *I've had quite a night.*

No! she responded. *But I'll get some!*

I don't remember doing it, but somehow in my pajamas, old lady glasses, and tangled mess of hair, I drove to her house. When I got there, I realized I'd somehow managed to put on deodorant and a bra, which was promising (and much appreciated).

When I walked in, there it was. An ornate bottle of tequila, presented on a plate with a pretty napkin in my usual chair at her table. A shot glass and lime wedge sitting next to it, waiting for me throw it back.

"Do it! Take a shot! We'll pick up your kids from school," they chanted. And so I did. Never in my life had I taken a shot of tequila, but right there in that moment and in the company of two of my best friends, I let go. I told them about my dear Sharon and my loss and sense of hopelessness, and they listened and hugged and encouraged me the way only true friends can and will.

It got me thinking about the importance of TRIBES. The birds of a feather. The people who take you as you are and overlook the pajamas, matted hair, and bloodshot eyes.

Over the next few hours we talked, cried, and must have gotten stirred into a real tizzy because, at some point that day, this book was born.

Several days later, I texted my friend, Kaley, who lives a few states away. I filled her in on all the details of the book Teri, Melissa, and I decided to author together. *With my local soul sisters*, I added to the text.

She replied: *Local? That's awesome! I wish I had soul sisters. I have some nice friends, but it's not the same.*

Well, it took me twelve years to find, I texted back. *We all need those friends who will take us in our PJs and give us a shot of tequila.*

I was sad for Kaley. I remember the loneliness I felt before these friends, and I know it can be tough. She's moved three times in the past five years. With so many moves and two young children, she has met plenty of friends. But there are always *people*. People who will keep you company or fill your calendar with lunch dates and coffee breaks. But people who ignite your soul and fill you up are the lucky pennies you stumble across at the exact moment you need a stroke of luck. And so you snatch them up and stuff them in your pocket to keep.

> Admit that motherhood can be lonely. It doesn't mean you want to give it up. It just means you want a friend.

Maybe you're reading this and feeling the same way. I'll tell you what I'd tell her.

It will come. Maybe you're in the season that feels like winter. While stowed away inside with cabin fever, newborn suckling on your breast and toddler attached to your hip, you focus on teaching them how to think and grow and experience the world, even though it seems to go on outside without you. Find peace in knowing you are exactly where you need to be and that this stage in life is temporary.

There will come a time when you get to step back outside again. And when you do, find your tribe.

They are not the ones with a bottle of superglue, hoping to fix your imperfect parts. They don't read the story of their lives to you like a fairy tale while you pretend yours is too. You will find each other in the mud. Both dirty and tired and able to admit it.

And you get in that mud by being brutally honest. Having courage. Baring your soul. Exposing the deepest parts of your heart to other women. Sometimes you have to filet yourself open and bleed out in front of someone else. As scary and vulnerable as that sounds, it's the only true form of connection that matters.

A tribe is defined as, "A group of distinct people, dependent on their land for their livelihood, who are largely self-sufficient and not integrated into the national society."

How so very apropos. We are dependent on our little tribe and the community in which we live to *thrive*. And there's room to find some humor in the fact that we're not fully integrated into the general society. We are our own breed. Our own blend. Our very own designer brand.

So when you find yourself in the promised season that finally allows you to explore the footage outside your winter cabin, go introduce yourself to your tribe and hold them close. Crowd around one another and show your battle scars, share your war stories, and shed some tears. Admit that motherhood can be lonely. It doesn't mean you want to give it up. It just means you want a friend. So let it all hang out and cling to the ones who shout, "Me too!" as they hand you a shot of tequila, ignore your bedhead, and help carry a heavy load. The stuff of magic exists in the muddy moments.

Those are the gals you want in your tribe.

TEMPER TANTRUM

Dear Dentist,

No, I am not going to brush my children's teeth, which may mean I am failing as a mother, but they are eight and ten years old. I barely have time to brush my own teeth. Which may mean I am just failing as a person.

Yours Truly,
#BadMom

14

THE WALL

by Melissa Rixon

I was dropping off the kids at school one morning when I saw her walking along the sidewalk with a kid grabbing each hand and a baby strapped to her chest. This frazzled mom was a reflection of who I've been so many times. Her hair was escaped her ball cap, and the children were bouncing and skipping and tugging on her rag doll arms and stepping on her toes while the flotsam and jetsam of their backpacks littered the ground around her. The baby had that constant look of surprise that babies tend to have, and this precious mom had that constant look of disbelief that mothers tend to have. The one that says, "I am walking in public in sweats I pulled out of the hamper. I don't even know myself anymore."

The window was rolled down in my car, and I briefly overheard her deflated tone when she passed a friend, "Is it seriously only Wednesday?" Her also disheveled friend nodded woefully as she dragged her own wiggling little boys down the sidewalk.

Oh, how many times have I been there. Clawing through to the weekend where the schedules are slightly less demanding and my husband is home to help with the heavy lifting. It feels like a little reprieve. Weekdays are hard! And they get even harder when life happens, as it tends to do, in all the space of all the days. Like accidentally oversleeping because one kid was up all night puking and the other one hasn't slept in his own bed for four nights in a row. Maybe you were fresh out of all the individual breakfast favorites and had to watch your children choke down pieces of toast while they groaned about whether there was too much butter or not enough butter or maybe it shouldn't have butter at all. Fashion is the last thing on your mind because there's no brain power to figure out an outfit that will cooperate with the extra five, ten, twenty-five pounds that nags you and reminds you of the workout you missed (again!) and how bad you suck at will-powering your way through a kitchen.

One kid needs a form signed for school. One needs new cleats by Monday. Somebody needs to be across town exactly five minutes after somebody else needs to be on the opposite side of town, and you're wondering how on earth you're going to split yourself in half to make it all work. Then, maybe, in the middle of it all, a car breaks down or a washing machine floods your newly remodeled kitchen or your credit card gets hijacked. Who has time to deal with the big things when the little things have snacked on your whole day?

A hundred miles an hour, diapers flying out the window, tires squealing, rubber burning . . . crash!

You hit the Wall. It's funny how it seems to pop up out of nowhere. How one minute you've got it together and the next minute you feel like you can't move a muscle. All your motivation leaks out on the floor, and suddenly everything stands still.

I'd love to say I can help you with this. That I have the answers and formulas, and the fix is some easy secret you just haven't uncovered yet. If that were the case, I'd give it away for free.

But the fact is that I don't know how to make your days easier or your nights more restful or your mornings more pleasant or your weeks less chaotic. I don't know how to make your kids more responsible or your husband more responsive. From what I can tell, there's no bag of tricks and nothing new to know.

But the Wall? Well, I do know a bit about that.

If you look closely at the bricks in the Wall you'll see words etched into them. Words like *overwhelm, chaos, rush, forget, postponed, defeat, exhaustion.* All the things we try to fix or escape. Perhaps we think that in order to escape we have to leap it in a single bound. It has to be easier! Serenity must exist *Over There.* And so we spend a lot of time trying to outsmart it.

I know every crack in the Wall. Every pin hole in it, letting light in from the other side. I know how wide it is because I've tried to go around it; I know how tall it is because I've tried to climb over it; and I know how hard it is because I've tried to chisel my way through it.

I can't show you the way to *Over There.*

But let me take a second and show you around *Over Here.*

On this side of the Wall, everything we treasure grows and flows deep and wide. It's where your children fall down and you help them get up again. It's where we go the distance by running in circles. On this side of the Wall are the tests and tribulations, the obstacles and timed trials. But there's some good news. The finish line is *Over Here* too. The moment I stopped looking for the prize on the other side is the moment I realized there was nothing to run from.

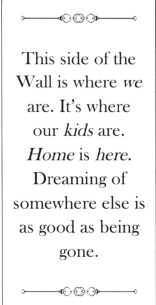

This side of the Wall is where *we* are. It's where our *kids* are. *Home* is *here.* Dreaming of somewhere else is as good as being gone.

You might have to push some things out of the way. You might have to tell someone, "No. I just can't today." You might have to take that money you were going to use to do something responsible and go on vacation instead, so you don't crumble. Maybe get a babysitter, so you can put on a dress, do your hair, have a date with your husband, and feel like a woman for a change. Perhaps accept the dusty coffee table for a few extra days if it means you can sit with the wind on your face for a few extra minutes.

This side of the Wall is where *we* are. It's where our *kids* are. *Home* is *here.* Looking anywhere but here is as good as being blind, and dreaming of somewhere else is as good as being gone. So snuggle in and make it comfortable. Decorate your place. Paint it your favorite shade of your favorite color, and plant some flowers here and there.

Because after a long day of worksheets and playground politics, our kids don't need to see mommy trying to escape.

One day we'll be on the other side. Because it turns out that *Over There* is just another word for *Empty Nest*. That's where our schedules are clear, our closets are neat, and the kitchen has enough food for two. We'll all be neighbors in *Empty Nest* one day.

But for now, I'm content living here, on this side of the Wall.

MELISSA'S MOTHERHOOD RESUME

Look what I can do . . .

- Manage tween hormones.

- Break up boy fights.

- Put throw pillows back on the couch. Again. And Again. (Help me!)

- Remember everyone's favorite everything: flavor, color, shoes, author, subject, dinner, and everything else.

- Clean pee off the floor. (I have two boys. 'Nuff said.)

- Create messy hair buns.

- Clean up dog hair.

- Shop the sale rack.

- Drink cold coffee.

- Locate a bad smell.

- Find a lost and dead phone.

- Overpack for trips.

- Assemble first-aid kits.

- Grant Christmas wishes.

- Bandage banged-up knees and elbows.

- Listen to bedtime prayers.

- Nag on school mornings. And all other mornings.

- Find the other shoe.

- Sculpt together dioramas.

- Rush forgotten items to school.

THINGS NO ONE TELLS YOU

Your Netflix belongs to your kids.

Your phone belongs to your kids.

Your food belongs to your kids.

Your lap belong to your kids.

Your bed belongs to your kids.

Your bathroom belongs to your kids.

Your entire existence and all that it entails
belongs to your kids.

You? Oh. Haha. There is no you.
There is just your **KIDS**.

15

CATCHING BUTTERFLIES

by Teri Mirikitani

As a life coach, one of the most common frustrations I hear from female clients is a feeling like they can't get anything done. In their moments of peace and quiet, a goal or dream will come to them and they say, "Yes, that sounds like a great idea. I'm going to do it!" Then the bubble of enlightenment bursts into a rainbow of colors, and they're back to reality, doing what they do best: putting their family first and themselves last.

Not long ago, I saw a guy on TV with an "act." He started on his unicycle and, one-by-one, his sparkly assistant tossed things at him to stack up and balance. He made it look easy. Take a chair! And he'd take the chair. A sword! A teacup! Something on fire! He wiggled on his unicycle with his things in the air, and I thought, *Hey, I can do that! Some things seem pointy, and some seem on fire. I have a balancing act too!*

There were times when I struggled with putting all my goals and dreams on hold, fearing I couldn't add one more thing on my motherhood unicycle. What happens if I drop one? Don't things blow up and burn down? Don't families suffer and kids eat cereal for dinner, and then Armageddon takes over the world?

There was simply no way I could risk failing at motherhood, because to fail at that meant I ultimately failed at everything.

So I let my dreams float by like butterflies. At first, it was a bit upsetting to watch them come and go, fluttering out of sight. But then, out of nowhere, if I had the time and a little extra gumption that day, I'd catch one. And a few days later, if the mood struck and my ducks were in a row, I'd reach out and catch a couple more. It wasn't some hard-hitting, multi-pronged attack. There weren't convoluted mission statements and five-year plans involved. It was just a little initiative here and there, and it slowly began to feel like progress. Because that's exactly what it was, even though it was much slower than thawing-molasses-in-the-heart-of-winter progress.

Then it hit me. I didn't need to sit around focusing on all the things I can't get done. I need to focus on feeling balanced. The best way to achieve that had nothing to do with saturating myself in my profession or motherhood or any one singular category. It meant not leaving things ignored and untouched for too long. And it meant not trying to hold them all at once on the unicycle.

> Just because you're the mom doesn't mean you can't feel a sense of accomplishment with your own goals and dreams. So go ahead. Give yourself a little nudge and an "Atta girl!"

Moms, putting your families first is a beautiful strength. It's not my intention to debunk that, because I believe in it too! To take your carefully crafted dreams and lay them aside for the sake of family is honorable and generous. But so often we do that when it's not required, and that's when it becomes a profound loss.

For so many moms, this superpower of unrelenting love for our families morphs into an unconditional sacrifice that kicks us square in the face and says, "There's no time for you right now." That will become our truth if we don't look this super-mom alter ego in the eye and say, "I'm taking a turn now, and you must be willing to share some time with me." We'll never get closer to achieving our dreams if we don't get a little tough with the Mothergeist who's taken us over.

Don't misunderstand. Being a great mom is a worthy purpose! But for that to be the one and only thing that defines us isn't growth. When things stay in one place for too long, they become stagnant, and that's not healthy at all.

To pursue our dreams is not *individualism*. This is *differentiation*. Individuation separates you from the whole, which undermines the nature of motherhood. Sometimes that is difficult for us to reconcile as women. But differentiation allows us to pursue goals and talents that are unique to us. It is so healthy for a family and marriage. Being challenged and completing tasks of our own give us a healthy dose of confidence and boosts our self-esteem, which is not only good for us but also for everyone around us.

Whether you're a stay-at-home mom, a work-from-home mom, a mom living the dream, or a mom working and parenting so much you've forgotten how to dream, maybe a little time spent on assessing your balancing act is necessary.

As for me and my first steps toward building a business, I became committed to making sure all areas of my life worked. I took inventory. Were my mornings running smoothly? Was I addressing my own physical wellness? Was there time in the afternoons to effectively deal with homework, chores, and running the kids to and from sports? Taking on anything new meant I needed to have a solid grip on the demands that already existed. For me, it meant moving a few things around. Merely changing the time of day I walked the dog or unloaded the dishwasher helped.

It turns out that I wasn't exceptionally out of balance or chaotic. I had assumed I had no time because I'd allowed motherhood to consume me!

So how do you get there? How do you flip the switch from all of one thing to some of everything? Try the following three steps.

Step One

We must understand that anything that lives in the extremes eventually fades or self-destructs. The adage, "You can have too much of a good thing," is true. That's why it's important to seek balance.

I had a client who was barely surviving on four hours of sleep. "Sleep is so vital! Why aren't you sleeping?" I asked with concern.

She began to list an excessive number of volunteer commitments at school, church, and kids' clubs. She'd stay up late organizing snacks for the team and get up early to cut items for the teacher's bulletin board. With a good heart, she'd run all day long helping anyone who would ask, and yet she felt unfulfilled and stressed out. In a moment of clarity, she realized she was unhappy, which lead her straight to me. Extremes, even in the case of this sweet well-intending mother, became her undoing.

Step Two

We need to be *very* specific on what we desire most and how that will make us feel. I suggest writing it down. Journal it daily. Claim it. Declare what you are going to be and how that will make you feel. Did you know that you are 40 percent more likely to achieve the things you take the time to write down? Those are decent odds when you consider it costs you nothing in terms of a real investment. And at the very least, you're clearing your head of thoughts swimming aimlessly in your mind.

Step Three

We need to get ready to deal with Self Doubt. She's the inner voice that shows up to bully you. To tell you that you're crazy for thinking you can because you'll never have the time. *You will most certainly fail*, she whispers. And, without wanting to, you listen to her. You're going to have to get firm with her. And then you're going to have to show her that she's out of line. A great way to do that is through the exercise of "Take Ten" (see page 47).

(see page 47)

―――――◦―◦⟨◦⟩―◦―――――

These three steps become your butterfly net. It allows you to capture your goals in tiny amounts. It won't catapult you or leap frog you or fast pitch you to any place strange and uncomfortable. It will simply and softly step you toward success.

Some days are better than others. The point is to try. There is no right or wrong. We are building a new habit, and habits have a way making our act on the unicycle a little less perilous. That guy on TV, with his swords and his fire, was a guy with a practiced habit.

Be kind to yourself as you begin this new practice. Frustration, self-judgement, and the fear of failure will make an appearance. But for your sake and the sake of your family, be resolute and determined to protect your *differentiation*.

You watch you children enjoy the feeling of accomplishment many times. Just because you're the mom doesn't mean you can't feel some of that too. So go ahead. Give yourself permission to move forward. Tell yourself, "Atta girl!" and then allow yourself to have fun. Enjoy catching those beautiful butterflies, a few at a time.

"For in every adult there dwells the child that was, and in every child there lies the adult that will be."

—John Connolly, *The Book of Lost Things*

16

SEEN, NOT HEARD

by Christi McGuire

My two sisters and I were raised by a single mom in a large extended family. We had a grandfather who owned his own company and did well, but because country bumpkin towns have a way of sliding a magnifying glass over things, he probably seemed more well-to-do and larger-than-life than he actually was.

Once in a while, we'd make the short journey to the neighboring town for a fancy dinner at the country club with Grandpa and the family. We'd slip into our best dresses, accessorized with our best behavior, and sit prim, proper, and delicately folded in our seats. My mother proudly accepted the praise for having such "well-mannered daughters."

I don't know if it was my own manners or the look on her face when they said it that made me feel proud. It was likely a combination of the two. But with curls in our hair and a touch of rouge on our chubby cheeks, we happily played princess for the better part of two hours, sitting still, chewing with our mouths closed, and smiling at the adults around us.

That glimpse into our childhood is the only thing that comes to mind when I try to understand this next story. The one where I found myself questioning how to raise my own daughters to be polite and yet still be tolerable people.

On the way to the mall one Saturday afternoon, my now adult sister and I took a detour through a Starbucks drive-through. My sister was driving, and therefore the one to place our order, and she quietly ordered for herself and then added my usual—a venti white chocolate mocha with whipped cream. The barista handed us our drinks at the window and was getting our change when I said, "Ask her for a stir stick."

My sister's head snapped to the right to get a look at me. "What? No!" she sputtered.

"Yes!" I said. "I like to stir in the whipped cream."

"No," she hissed. "I can't do that."

"Yes!" I was a twelve-year-old again, tangling with my sister. "Just ask for the freakin' stir stick!"

"No!" she yelled back, ever the stubborn one, and sped away without her change.

I could see my face in the side rearview mirror. It was twisted with horror, confusion, and shock.

Embarrassment and lack of confidence were the two crippling culprits at the root of her withering. She was still unintentionally holding to the insufferable mantra, "Children should be seen and not heard." Only she was an adult now, one who needs to be heard if she hopes to be happy. She has a beautiful soul with a smile to match, but sitting still and being pretty isn't always enough.

In fact, it's often not even close.

I've never suffered from this. Those who know me well probably chuckled when they read that. Maybe it is being the first born, but I've never been a wilting rose in any setting for any reason. I've spoken my mind and asserted myself, and so it's hard for me to empathize with people who don't speak up. Watching my own sister fall into that sort of nonsense had me completely undone.

As a result, I've diligently spent the years since that incident fulfilling my sisterly obligation of reminding her of that moment each and every time she hints at something that requires a little too much nerve or might demand a little of her spine. Not in a mean-spirited sense, of course, but in the encouraging-older-sister way, and she seems to be getting better at speaking up more and placing more value on her own needs.

And it's helped to shed some light on how I attempt to raise my girls. I like etiquette as much as the next mother, and I get that same sense of pride when strangers compliment their table manners. But I also teach them about being a conversationalist. To say interesting things and listen well and find common topics to talk about, whether they are chatting with their four-year-old cousin or their ninety-four-year-old great-grandmother. To speak up for themselves, whether it is to ask for a straw or a napkin or to please leave the cherry off the milkshake. Or perhaps to approach their teachers about unanswered questions or extra credit or the bully on the playground.

My husband and I have encouraged them order their own meals at restaurants since they were old enough to talk. We have worked with them to look the waiter or waitress in the eye, to speak clearly, and to order their own meals, politely but assertively. My younger daughter would refuse many times—sometimes she was shy and other times stubborn—so it's taken several years to work with her. But now she speaks up and is proud of herself for being able to order *both* honey mustard and ranch dressing for her chicken fingers. Sometimes, the waitress ignores the children and looks to me to respond. I smile and say, "They can order for themselves." And they can. They are human beings, and even at nine and eleven years old, they are capable of participating in and contributing to society.

Ordering chicken fingers and extra sauce may seem insignificant, but once my girls felt confident in doing this, they moved on to bigger, harder tasks. Such as standing up in the school cafeteria, taking their trays, and moving next to the kid who is bashful and sits alone at the end of the lunch table. Like gently saying to a friend, "I'm sorry, but we don't treat one another like that. We need to be kind to one another and let everyone play this game."

It's not all or nothing. You don't have to choose between being brash and nasty or lying down in the road. That's where we should all strive to be. Exercising confidence and executing it with politeness and a winning smile.

Because whether we need a stir stick or simply need to stir things up, little girls and big girls alike, deserve to be seen *and* heard.

TEMPER TANTRUM

Do you have to?

YES.

Yes, you have to go to bed tonight.

Like you do every night.

Yes, you have to brush your teeth.

Like you do every day.

Yes, you have to eat your vegetables.

Like you do at every dinner.

JUST DO IT!

17

THE HOUSE THAT MATTER BUILT

by Melissa Rixon

There's an unassuming house. It's hidden and it's small. Pretense doesn't touch it. Elements don't rattle it. The floor creaks a bit. And the door. And the stairs. The walls are full of fingerprints. The furniture well worn. It's a place that's built for safety. It is happy. It's secure.

When my son Michael was about two years old, I took him to the pediatrician for an annual checkup and was sure to point to a rather large freckle that had formed on his scalp, just inside his hairline.

"Well, we don't need to do anything about that now, but watch it," the doctor explained. "If it hasn't gone away by the time he's about twelve, then we'll remove it."

"Twelve?" I asked. "His hair is gonna grow in thick, and I won't see it anymore. I hope I don't forget."

"You won't forget." He continued listening to Michael's heart and checking his reflexes.

"I don't know, doctor," I said. "Just today I forgot my insurance card, and yesterday I forgot to feed the dog. I feel like I'm better at forgetting everything than remembering anything at all these days."

He stopped and smiled at me. "You'll see. That's just the sort of thing moms don't forget. Moms don't forget the stuff that matters."

Michael is now eleven-and-a-half. And I haven't forgotten that I need to bring up the freckle to the doctor at his well-visit appointment in a few months. Even though it's barely there anymore. Even though I didn't set an alarm ten years ago. Even though I haven't written it down in a calendar every year for a decade. Just because the doctor was right—mothers don't forget the things that matter.

We might forget to do our hair or order new checkbooks, file our nails or water the gardenias, but we don't forget birthdays or hugs and kisses or prayers or dinner. And we don't forget ten-year-in-advance appointments we make with our kid's pediatrician. The *matterings* of life are right there in our wheelhouses.

The scientific definition of *matter* is "something that takes up physical space." This can be your purse, your car, your earrings, you, your dog, all the Barbie shoes in the entire world, and, as evidenced by balloons, it can even be air.

As a lover of language, I really dig the fact that when something takes up space

> Your *Matter House* is the most important place in the world. It's the place for things that matter and the place for no matter whats. The world is a better place because of your *Matter House.*

in our hearts and spirits, we also call it *matter*. Even though science decidedly doesn't acknowledge it as such.

Matters of mothering defy science, though. We don't confine things to a space; we expand to give them more of it.

How many times have you volunteered to do something for school, church, sports, or music? The things nobody else wanted to do because they didn't have time—and neither do you. But you do it because deep down in this place that burns warm and bright inside you, a place no scientist will ever prove or disprove, is your Matter House.

It's the place you consult when you're buying character Band-Aids or painstakingly constructing a weekly menu with all the finicky considerations of the preschooler you cook for. It's that place that navigates your daughter's hurt feelings or your son's first crush or your baby's first steps. It's the place that gives you the strength to finish the day, bedraggled and frazzled and completely emptied out, but confident you did your best even when your best sort of sucked at times.

It's so important, your Matter House. Maybe the most important place in the world. The place for things that matter and the place for no matter whats.

No matter what, I love you.
No matter what, I'll be there.
No matter what, I'll do it. I'll give it. I'll get it.
I'll fix it. I'll kiss it. I'll make it better somehow.

And it does make it better. It makes so many things better. As a result, the world is then better. All because of your Matter House. It's the place that assigns value to people and causes and children and movements. It provides a safe haven for the sick and afflicted. It's the place that pushes over and under, on, around, and through, whatever is required when and where. It's the place that gives you the gumption to go. To be. To do. To stand.

It's also the place that God built. It's the place where God lives, I think. And it's been inside women since the beginning of time. That space of warmth that smells like autumn and feels like Christmas and spreads peace, hope, and security all over the world.

Sometimes, from the inside, it feels like a mess, as it shifts and groans under the pressure of a straining job. But that's exactly what it looks and sounds like to build something out of love. It looks war-torn and weary because love is a mighty fighter. We shore it up and patch where we need it, fortify, add on, and expand.

It's work, yes. But it's a content work. A bold, beautiful, and worthy work.

What's in your Matter House?

Is that where you store your kids' favorite colors? Maybe their favorite meals, so when they've had a bad day you can serve up a heaping helping of comfort on a plate made just for them. Maybe it's their favorite flavor of popsicles for when they're sick or the uniforms they need washed before the big game. Maybe it's the teacher conference or the new food intolerance or the challenging math concept that requires a tutor.

Maybe it's just a hug. Maybe it's a voice reminding you to stop and give that hug even when you're running late or when your to-do list wraps around the earth.

Take a peek inside your Matter House.

There's an unassuming house. It's hidden and it's small. Pretense doesn't touch it. Elements don't rattle it. The floor creaks a bit. And the door. And the stairs. The walls are full of fingerprints. The furniture well worn. It's a place that's built for safety. It is happy. It's secure.

THINGS NO ONE TELLS YOU

Weeknights are for kid stuff.
Weekends are for more kid stuff.

When you want to remove your child from a setting he does not wish to leave, he has the ability to shift into an oozy, shapeless mess, which is impossible to hold, grab, carry, or control. The one and only medicine for this is a solid bribe.

Bribery is a tricky medium in parenthood. It must be rare, effective, possible, and worth it.

If the package of something new boasts that it cannot be broken, it will still be broken in ways beyond the possibilities of repair.

If you have something new, go ahead and have your kid wipe her chocolate face on it. It just gets all that stress out of the way.

Your child will lovingly point out your bad breath and the thing in your teeth. He'll ask if your non-pregnant friend is pregnant or talk about that one time you passed gas. And he'll do it all in front of an audience.

18

A TRUE FRIEND

by Teri Mirikitani

Did you know one of the major complaints among mothers is that they're lonely? Imagine that. A house full of people and yet they feel alone. It doesn't surprise me to hear that, really. I've felt that loneliness from time to time as well. Especially during the baby and toddler years.

It's in those moments we realize we could use a friend. I'm not speaking of your kids or your husband or your sister or your child's teacher. These aren't the people you run into at the grocery store or who like your Facebook posts.

I'm talking about a friend. *A true friend.*

It's no secret that a good one can be hard to find.

I don't know why we women tend to be so hard on one another. Why we find it difficult to celebrate each other and root for one another's success. Maybe it's because we're insecure. Because if someone else is doing a better job, then we'll feel like we're getting it all wrong. As if someone else's success shines a spotlight on our mediocrity or failures.

I've known women who avoid other women altogether in order to avoid that feeling. Because they don't want to be alone or feel left out. Likewise, I've known women who've tolerated bad friends far too long, simply because they're tired of feeling lonely. But I propose to you that you can find good friends—and you deserve them. Maybe you've been caught in the snag of crummy friendships for so long you've forgotten what *true* friendship looks like. Allow me to share some of the many faces a true friend may look like.

A true friend gets how hard you try every day, even though your home is something Martha Stewart would condemn. She sees the dust bunnies playing house in the corner of your living room, and she just looks the other way, unfazed and understanding. She doesn't care if your dishes are done or if there are toys scattered all over the kitchen or there's dust on your bookcase. Wherever she stands is a judgement-free zone.

Three days in your sweats, with your hair thrown up in a pony-bun-knot-combo, and you're not even sure she notices your fashion nightmare. Not because she doesn't *care* enough to notice, but because she cares *so* much she doesn't *see* it.

When your days are good, she's there to celebrate. And when your days are bad, she's there to highlight all the beautiful things about you . . . your smile, easy disposition, great sense of humor, wit, positive perspective, and ability to uplift her mood. The way you make her see the brighter side of things, no matter how dark the reality may appear.

She's eager to roll up her sleeves and find solutions to any obstacles that challenge your way to triumphs big and small. She's there to brainstorm and focus on possibilities, not pitfalls, so that Lady Creativity shines brightly on you as you make a long list of "what could be" if you only tried. And she always, always leaves you with a sense of release and lightheartedness when you part!

She's your cheerleader, your positive spin, and your Little Engine That Could, who won't let you think of yourself as anything other than a winner. Even when you're deep in the tunnels of life with darkness on both ends, hers is the voice of promise, "You're almost there. Keep going!"

She points out your children's good manners and pleasant faces and describes how she is witness to the way your children lovingly smile at you, how they hug you in public, and how they honor and prove the amazing mother you are, even when you feel like you are the worst. When your angelic child is replaced by the spawn of the devil in a hormonal fit of rage, your friend is confident in the passing of those moods, and her confidence makes you breathe a little easier too. She'll snap you out of it by saying, "The days are long, but the years pass swiftly. Ages and stages." And then she'll offer up ideas to take off the edge.

Whining about not having done one thing for yourself in months? She won't think you a malcontent and disapprove of your attitude. She'll just smile and comfort you.

She'll let you groan about your husband without questioning the strength of your marriage, and she'll listen to you complain about your schedule without blaming you for committing to it.

Need a little vacation from the daily grind? Dinner, some wine, and a movie leave you giddy with a sense of freedom and escapism while you laugh and tell silly stories and make great confessions and bask in the cozy presence of her friendship for a while.

She's the one you can be vulnerable with, because she'd never betray your confidence. She's your confessor and, without a doubt, she's a vault. It's not her story to tell, so she doesn't pass it on.

You can share the hopes and dreams of who you want to be when you finally get your chance, and she'll see the dream light up in you and say, "I see it! It's happening! I can't wait to watch it all unfold!"

She's not a gossip, because who needs to put other people down to feel better? Together, you'll take whatever is down and shine it up. Pull weeds and plant beautiful flowers. Laugh about failure because that's where the lessons lie.

She'll never let you put yourself down because you are too precious to her to think that way about yourself. She wouldn't stand for that kind of talk about you from others—certainly not out of your own mouth!

She's the low-maintenance friend. No expectations, no pressure, no nagging phone calls, no guilt, and no manipulation. She respects all your obligations, especially to your family. She'll take whatever time you can give her, whenever you can give it, and that is more than enough.

Some people enjoy the amusement of "brutal honesty" and present what often feels like a blatant put-down to you as if it's a gift. *That's a dumb idea. Why would you do that? That won't work.* But not this friend. Even her truth feels like a hug because it's spoken in love. And anything spoken in love is warm in the center.

She's not possessive of you. She easily shares you with others because your friendship is not something she wants to keep in a cage. She wants everyone to enjoy the gift she finds in you.

She's a breath of fresh air on a stale day. She makes the loads feel lighter. She's your shot in the arm when you need a boost. She is kind, respectful, caring, admirable, inspiring, and encouraging. She's a comedian and a vindicator. There is nothing superficial, forced, or contrived.

***

Do you have a friend like that? If you do, then you're one of the lucky ones. If you've thought of someone special as you've read this, then continue to deeply care for that friendship. Make it a priority. It's a rare and precious gift, and it belongs treasured in that place you save for rare and precious things.

And if you don't . . . if you've been reading and feeling a sense of something missing, don't worry. You're not alone.

You need to get creative with your interests and then go there. Find a class or join a club. Like minds congregate, and you will find a person who has something in common with you. Friendships build on common ground. At the very least, you will be stimulating your need for discovery.

Your community is crawling with women who may feel the same way. They want to connect and to be heard. Talk to them, listen to them, ask them to coffee. You don't need to host a party or go to a fancy restaurant. Your local café has a table for growing friendships.

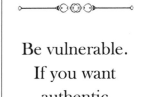

Be vulnerable. If you want authentic relationships with others, you must be you. Reveal your true self.

Be vulnerable. If you want authentic relationships with others, you must be you. This is not the time for your dolled-up version or your edited version or the version you keep under wraps. This is a time to reveal your true self. And you will receive that version of them in return.

There are hundreds of women wandering the parks, grocery stores, and Facebook who are just like you, who are looking for a friend. A true friend. Start here if this feels more comfortable. This is who you want to find, yes. But this is also who you should *be*. So be this. Be this and you will find this. It's that easy. Friends attract friends. They're like great, big, warm and fuzzy magnets. When you find each other, you'll know. In the precious words of Nancy Spain, "There are those you love immediately and forever."

Go find your forever friend. She's been waiting just for you.

"My mom has made it possible for me to be who I am. Our family is everything. Her greatest skill was encouraging me to find my own person and own independence."

—Charlize Theron

19

TO THINE OWN SELF BE TRUE

by Christi McGuire

I want to be a Broadway star in my normal, everyday life. I'm a sucker for people frolicking on stage and singing about nothing. How much more exciting would it be to make dinner if I could turn the whole humdrum ordeal into a song and dance routine while I wore something low cut, bold, and bedazzling?

Until recently, *Joseph and the Amazing Technicolor Dreamcoat* was my all-time favorite show. I saw it for the first time years ago, when Donny Osmond played Joseph. Wowza. DONNY. I was an eighteen-year-old girl on a school field trip, and all at once I was in love with musicals, muscles, and dreamy lead actors with dark hair and bare chests.

A short time ago, I stumbled upon another fabulous show, *Something Rotten*, which is based on Shakespeare and another talented and aspiring playwright named Nick Bottom. Nick is so green with envy and consumed with an obsession of stealing Shakespeare's spotlight that he begins spying and copying his in-the-works works of art.

I was immediately reeled into the fabulous and funky songs and quick-witted dialogue (in my forties, the things that stimulate me have changed a bit). But there was something more to it that spoke to me. And here's the weird part. It spoke to the *mom* part of me. It was Nick Bottom. His inability to see his ability, his unwillingness to acknowledge his own talent, his desperate need to be someone else because he couldn't stop comparing himself *to* someone else.

Just that week, I'd taken a break from Facebook. It's not that I don't enjoy my friends there. I do. I love to see the pictures of their kids, their vacations . . . even their perfectly plated bowl of spaghetti. But I struggle with those same things too. I tend to compare myself. Get down on myself.

"I wish I could take MY kids to Spain."

"Why didn't MY daughter know how to do algebra in Pre-K?"

"Why does MY spaghetti look a little bit like cat puke?"

It's hard not to get the drearies when you're cleaning pee off the toilet seat and you see that your friend *Just had to rush out of the house for the housekeeper! Hair still wet. #notime.*

Or you've just hung your kid's B+ on the fridge in time to read *Little Johnny just got recruited for Duke Summer Camp! #brainsfordays #smarterthanme.*

Deep down, these things can prick at our insecurities and make us feel like we're doing no good.

Maybe it's not social media. Perhaps it's the super chiseled, never ruffled mom you see at school drop off. She's cool and shiny with her fresh manicure and skinny latte. She's just dropped off

>
>
> We became entranced with the picture of perfect that blindsided us on the sidewalk.

a bag of donations for the classroom treasure chest, and she's off to pick up her husband's dry cleaning, after chatting with her friend about making her own kombucha. And you're all like, "I'm so lame. I don't even know what *kombucha* is."

Somewhere, we lose sight of it all. We didn't even feel the tight hug our daughter gave us before she skipped off to class. We're not even sure we told her to have a nice day. We became entranced with the picture of perfect that blindsided us on the sidewalk. We don't realize that, to our own kiddos, we are Broadway stars. We rock their world. Every single day. (Or at least *most* days.) But, for whatever reason, we only see how someone else's star is shining, whereas ours looks dull and pathetic.

Why do we do this to ourselves?

Why do we assume this is a zero-sum game? If someone else is doing well, does that mean we suck? If someone else has a smart kid, does that mean we don't?

We must stop.

For starters, all you see in anybody or on anybody is what they allow you to see. Do you get that? Do you know that everything someone shares on social media is what they have edited and filtered for your eyes. You don't see the rough draft, unless they think it's good enough (which usually never is). You don't see the mess in the background, unless they post the picture of it. We know this because this is how we share ourselves with the world too!

Yet, we are too busy gawking at other's filtered perfection to appreciate our own full and beautiful selves. Who we've become. What we've accomplished, whether it was changing a diaper or being promoted to CEO.

It's time to stop it. *Stop it!* Instead of allowing someone else's edited version of her life get you down, take a moment to give her a nod of "well done" and then move on. If it inspires you, so be it. If it motivates you? Fine. If it makes you feel less than, downtrodden, woe is me, or suckage, then you must walk away.

In the play, Nick Bottom thinks he hates Shakespeare. But after some careful consideration, he admits he really wants to *be* Shakespeare, at which point he is encouraged by his brother (in the words of the Bard himself), "To thine own self be true."

Maybe we also need to remember that here in Mommy-ville, where Pinterest turns us into catty crafters and Facebook sets our standard of achievement. Let's just be awesomely ourselves. In all phases and stages of motherhood. Let's get real, be true, and then sing and dance about it all in the kitchen.

You can even share it on Instagram, if you like.

TEMPER TANTRUM

"Mom, can you hold this?"

"Mom, can you sign this?"

"Mom, can you open this?"

No! Because I'm DRIVING!

20

PITY PARTY

by Melissa Rixon

I look around and notice everything wrong. The late afternoon sun brings out the yellow hue of the pollen film sticking to everything standing still on the patio. There's debris on the bottom of the pool that hasn't been swept in days. I stir it around with my toe, thinking of a most unpleasant way to bring it to my husband's attention. I'm barely propped up on the only raft that holds any air, but I'm pretty sure there's a slow leak.

I hear music coming from inside the house. I hear laughter and merry making. My husband, Matt, is singing loudly. Our three kids are hysterical. *Listen to them egging him on,* I think. *They are having a good time. And I am the cranky, old mom in the pool who doesn't belong. The outcast. Always serious, woeful, and a total drag.*

As the sun hands the day to the moon, dusk creeps in. A tall group of four palm trees in one corner of my yard catches my eye. *They look happy,* I think, as their fronds wiggle in the breeze. Their stature makes them look proud. *Well, that one looks like Matt, and there's Madeline. And there's Merrick. And that fourth one is Michael. All standing together tall, happy, and proud. And where am I? Of course, I'm not one of them.* I cry and sip the wine I'd poured from a bottle that had been open almost two weeks. It's hard to swallow, but I will it down.

My sights settle on the sick and withered grapefruit tree in the other corner of the yard. Separated from those cheerful, stoic palms. Half bent over and struggling to survive.

Oh, there I am, I think. *I am the bitter and bent-over grapefruit tree. Alone in the corner yard where no one will touch it.*

<hr />

It had been a *fine* weekend. (You're supposed to read "fine" the way you'd imagine a hormonal teenager saying it. *Fine.* It was *fine.* Like that.) We'd just come back from spending the day at my parents' house, where my mom happily had shown off her new plantation shutters and freshly remodeled kitchen. I marveled at the way it all sparkled and took deep breaths full of fresh paint. It was so clean and put together—no stain, spot, or Lego minefield in sight.

But then we came home to *my* house, and the smell of old garbage kicked us in the teeth when we walked in. The dog had gotten into the kitchen trash can again and carefully shredded and scattered everything in it all over the house. We stood there surveying the damage—the smell, the mess, the whining sound the dog was making from under the dining room table. For good measure, there was pile of puke nearby him. Something he'd no doubt eaten from the trash a little too eagerly.

"Well, I guess we should get started on this," my husband said, gesturing at the carnage and grabbing a broom.

But I couldn't. All of a sudden, I just couldn't do any of it anymore. "Why bother?" I spat the words like poison. The fact was, I'd just come from a perfect and always presentable house, and I'd spent the entire ride home quietly thinking of that and how just being inside it had made me feel like a failure.

"Your mom doesn't have kids at home anymore," my husband had said. "Of course it's clean."

"It was always clean," I'd managed to whisper. "Her house has always looked like that. Even when she had kids at home and was working full time and finishing a PhD, it looked like that. I can't even handle making lunch without the house falling to pieces while I do it." Then my voice was gradually carried away. The rest of the ride home had been silent, until we were delivered into the depths of ruin that was our living room.

Staring into the thick it, I lost myself. Suddenly, everything felt personal. The kids' shoes in the middle of the floor, an empty Capri Sun straw wrapper, the coffee grounds the dog had tracked around the hallway in what appeared to be very joyful circles.

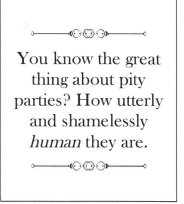

You know the great thing about pity parties? How utterly and shamelessly *human* they are.

"This is no different from any other day!" I yelled. "Maybe we should thank the dog for making the sty so inviting for the pigs who live here. It's like he's saying 'Welcome Home'!"

Matt and I ended up at each other's throats, saying things we didn't mean, until I'd had enough and sulked out to the swimming pool with a glass of stale Moscato. Which is precisely where I proceeded to throw myself an epic party. Theme? *Pity.*

I sip my wine, I cry, and I lie in the pool for hours on a slowly deflating raft. It's a whole scene. I think about my mom's kitchen and how she so easily parted with the one I grew up in and replaced it with shiny and pretty and everything new. It makes me feel strangely discarded and desperate for something shiny and new at a time when everything I own is covered in other people's fingerprints and boogers. I feel desperate for a place that feels like the model home in the magazines. Because try as I might, I can't seem to make my own home feel like that.

Mine sounds, smells, and looks like chickens should be roosting in it, I think. *Oh, what's that over there? Behind the couch? You know. Those are just chickens.*

It's getting dark, so Matt flips on the pool light for me. He must have peeked out to see me floating alone, forlorn and dramatic in the dark, but was unwilling to interrupt my melancholy soak. *Marriage can be really hilarious.*

I look down to find that I am nearly sunk. My raft has almost entirely deflated. *I am like this raft,* I think. *Deflated and sinking under the behemoth weight of the world. I am the raft. I am the grapefruit tree. I am my mother's old kitchen, just not even good enough anymore.*

There is no shortage of metaphors for my pathetic station in life.

But there's something creepy about being alone in a pool after dark, even with a light flipped on. So I wade out and wrap myself in a towel Matt has left by the door.

—◇◇◇—

You know the great thing about pity parties? How utterly and shamelessly *human* they are. If you're gonna throw one, you might as well go all out. Be generous with it. Give it room and give it gas and fire up all the music of the world's tiniest violins.

There must be buckets of tears. Really turn on the spigot. If you're like me and you don't cry often, then use it as an opportunity to really wring it out. Your family and all the onlookers are not going to be any more perplexed by your gallon of tears than they will be by a teacup full, so let 'em drip down your face and off your chin until they form rivers into and out of your soul. There is no limit to how many things you can carry on about. Big things, little things, historic things, recent things, major, minor—waller in the minutia. All those things you swallow down and button up for the sake of propriety . . . this is when you let it all hang out. There are no chaperones, no scripts, and no other guests.

There is just one rule.

Like any good party, if you're having a helluva time, it's easy to overstay your welcome. But etiquette demands that we don't, and so does our sanity.

At some point, you have to clean up the mess. You have to get out of the pool, throw away the broken raft, and bid adieu to the sad grapefruit tree and the family of palms. You have to dry off with the towel your husband leaves by the door, walk in, and take part in a silly family singing and dancing before you call your mom and tell her you love her new kitchen. And then you have to roll up your sleeves and clean up your own kitchen.

You have to reconcile within yourself so many things. If how we experience life is a direct result of our own expectations, then perhaps happiness requires some remodeling on the *inside* of us. Maybe we stop comparing ourselves to others who look like they do

142

it better and stop wishing our two-year-olds would act like ten-year-olds. Stop convincing ourselves the dog got in the trash on purpose and that the produce rotted in the fridge because we can't do anything right.

At some point, our peace demands that we stop taking everything so personally. Because in truth, almost nothing ever is.

Cry your tears, Mama. It cleanses your soul. But then dry your eyes, fix your mascara, and get back in the game. You're the only one who can do this job, so walk in like a boss and have at it.

"The fastest way to break the cycle of perfectionism and become a fearless mother is to give up the idea of doing it perfectly—indeed to embrace uncertainty and imperfection."

—Arianna Huffington

21

NO ANNUAL REVIEW

by Teri Mirikitani

I stirred the shredded chicken in the Crock-Pot, closed out a client file, and headed to the ball field. I saw lightening, then heard thunder. In typical Florida fashion, a monsoon swooped in just in time to drench me as I got my son from the dugout. It was the bitter end of a tired and frustrating day. I'd worn all the mom hats: the grocery getter, the homework tutor, the resident nurse, and the personal chef. All the while juggling the job that pays me money. The end was near, but to get there I still had to don the cabbie hat and collect my kids from their various activities.

The storm persisted as I picked up my daughter from soccer, drove home, and raced into the house, only to race back out to the car because she was clearly going to suffocate and possibly die a horrible teenage death without the phone she left inside it.

Exhausted, cranky, and wet, I spent the better part of the next thirty minutes listening to my kids bicker about everything and nothing. I tried to ignore it, too drained to get involved, but finally attempted to break it up with some minor requests.

"Alise, I need you to take your backpack upstairs. Nolan, I need you to clean up your mess in the den." I darted to my own room to hang up my jacket and came back to find them still engaged in the tit-for-tat nonsense. Not even a glimmer of acknowledgment of my requests. Not even a millimeter of movement toward completing the simple, everyday chores.

My eyes bulged.

"Kids . . ." I interrupted slowly, attempting to maintain my self-control. "I need you to take care of these things. *Right now.*"

Still no reply. Instead, they dug their heels deeper into the ground they were holding. Invisible, I was a ghost on the outside. A mere figment of my own imagination.

Frustration began bubbling in the core of my being, smothered what little self-control I had left, and spewed out all over the floor. My typically angelic teenage daughter and I locked eyes and drew swords. Between gritted teeth, my words came out slowly and staccato-like, punching the air that hung between us: "I just need a little respect. And a little appreciation and cooperation. I bleed out every day. Every. Single. Day. And for whom? For you guys. For all the people who just come, sit at my feet, and ask for more and more and more. And you know what? I don't have any more to give. I. am. done."

Alise's eyes narrowed, and her long, dark ponytail wagged as she tilted her head to one side and unleashed her own fury. "Well, I didn't know you were so unhappy being a mom! Why don't you just get a real job? Like one in an office?"

In that split second of time, the earth stopped spinning. The clock stopped ticking. Time froze, and everything went black and empty and silent. Except for those words clanging around and echoing in the deepest parts of me.

My cheek stung from her verbal slap in the face.

My shoulders slumped as I took in her words, her expression. We're finding new ground, she and I. She's saying what she means, and I encourage her to do so, but sometimes the things we mean to say sting, and her stinger was stuck in my chest. But I know my daughter. She wasn't being mean; she was being thirteen. And so I inhaled deeply and made an effort to explain myself.

"I could, Alise. I could get a *real* job, and maybe I should. Maybe I'm just too available. Maybe I've done you and your brother a disservice in the long run, because I've made you feel like none of this comes at a price. You know nothing of not being able to play the sport you want because your parents can't manage the schedule. Or having to make your own breakfast in the morning because I'm already gone. Or buying your lunch every day, hitching rides with friends, doing your own laundry, or sharing the load of cleaning the house. All the things that my 'not-a-real-job' demands of me, demands nothing of you, except a little respect. And if that's too much to ask, then maybe I am misplacing my time. I'll begin looking tomorrow. For a job in an office. Away from home. And you should take some time to think about the batch of inconveniences and sacrifices this will impose on all of us."

Completely unaware to the both of us, my eleven-year-old son had been sidelining quietly with eyes as big as super moons. The monologue I'd delivered to his sister had ballooned into a giant threat in his chest. "No, Mommy! You can't! You can't get a job! Please! I love everything you do around here. I think it's really great. And look! I'm cleaning up the den right now. As a matter of fact, I'll even clean something else. Like these shoes. Whose are these shoes, anyway? It doesn't matter. I'll clean them up right now."

I chuckled a little at his desperation and put my eyes back on my daughter. This delightful girl, my biggest fan and most passionate cheerleader. She didn't understand. How could she? Life has not demanded it of her . . . yet. And I realized therein lies the mission.

At that moment, my heart pulled tightly for both of us. One day she would probably be a mother like me, finding that place in the world where we exist as both a mom and a woman. Maybe one with a hotshot career. Maybe as a stay-at-home mom. Or just maybe trying to do both at once, like me. Who knows?

"Ya know, Alise. There's something I miss about having an office job. Sure, I work independently from home. But what about my *job* as your mom? I don't miss the rat race or even the steady paycheck. It's the annual review. You go to school, and you work hard, and you get good grades. And that report card comes home, and you feel good. You see the sum of your efforts printed onto a paper that you can show your parents, who are then also proud. It's this whole cycle of encouragement and reward. I used to get that too. At a *real* job. Once a year, the boss would sit down and go over my performance and give me a raise for a job well done, and it felt good. Having my effort evaluated and acknowledged meant I wasn't invisible. That the hours I put into a day added up to something. I don't get that any more. Nobody reviews my job at all, particularly my life's work as your mother. And just now you made me realize it's because you don't even see mothering as a job. But it is. And I think it's the most important job of all. Being *here*. And being *there* for you and your brother. Your dad thinks it's important too, which is why he also supports the idea of it. But sometimes—I'm not gonna lie—I feel very insignificant, which is hurtful because it's truly the most significant portion of my life. I hope one day you figure out a way around that feeling, because I wish for more than that for you."

She sauntered up the stairs, belongings in hand. Later, I heard her shower, and after that I heard the last steps her bedtime routine.

> We will never get a more accurate annual review than one that offers a true reflection of self. And our kids are our perfect mirrors.

I sat down, a bit startled by the unfolding events of the evening, and asked myself hard questions. *Am I unhappy with what I'm doing? Should I find something else?*

The truth is that some days I wish I wasn't Mrs. Flexibility. I'd look at my husband, always clearly focused. Ironically, there seems to be freedom in his orderly days and well-defined next steps, and there sure is freedom at home in the evenings, when he's left work for the relaxing calm of our living room. He's kicked back, watching ESPN, with his shoes off while I'm still locked in overdrive, making dinner, prepping backpacks, and checking schedules for the next day. My job as a life coach is flexible, and flexible people tend to carry the most.

Maybe if I went to an office job, I'd get to feel the peace of time off. Something I've not felt in . . . well, about thirteen years.

I heard the soft thuds of Alise making her way back down the stairs. Her eyes, downcast and awash in introspection, were saturated in regret. "I'm sorry, Mom," she said. "I don't know why I said all that."

All of a sudden, there it was. My teenage daughter, unprovoked and deeply sincere, was sorry. A striking revelation came with it.

Motherhood is a job that doesn't come with pats on the back, pay raises, or a cheerleading squad. It comes with its own form of proof of a job well done.

The moms who work outside the home don't necessarily have to go digging around to find proof they're good at something. That's something a little harder to find for those of us who stay home. Likewise, I've heard working moms question their effectiveness on the family end of things. As if they're afraid they're missing too much and leaving some sort of negative imprint on their children as a result. And to all of that, all the second-guessing and self-doubting, I say this . . .

Do you have a baby who is finally sleeping through the night? Do you have a potty-trained toddler? Do you have a second-grader who can read? Or a fifth-grader who can clean his room? Do you have child who can add and subtract or go to school and be respectful to the teacher? Do you have a kid who can tie her shoes or complete a puzzle or say please and thank you? Do you have a child who can *apologize*?

This is the sum of our days. Our life's work. We are teaching a human being to *be human*. By teaching our kids to think for themselves, to put thoughts into action, to strive for their ideals and dreams, to try again when they fail, to be responsible and kind—it means that we've modeled all of that for them. We will never get a more accurate annual review than one that offers a true reflection of self. And our kids are our perfect mirrors.

Let a sense of pride wash over you as you consider this. You've earned a moment to bask in the sunlight of your accomplishment, so sit back and enjoy it. It's entirely possible you may be back in the rain tomorrow.

TEMPER TANTRUM

The nightly beauty regime. Because it takes thirty-nine minutes, three jars, two tubes, four lotions, and one tub of coconut oil to make me look this tired.

22

I WANT MY MOM

by Christi McGuire

It was a plague of biblical proportions. There were fevers, there were chills, there were aches, and there were pains. Sneezing, wheezing, and coughing reverberated throughout each room of my house. Every other hour, the scourge claimed another healthy victim who buried themselves under a blanket and passed out.

The last man standing? Me.

So I did what moms do. Armed with Lysol, Ibuprofen, a digital thermometer, and enough homemade soup to feed a small country, I tended every groan and whimper. I actively worked to disinfect everything every time it was touched by these sick beings draped on couches like rag dolls and zombies. I rapidly changed and sanitized bedding as I urged my three invalids to hydrate, hydrate, hydrate.

There were still chores to be done, as well, of course. Inside the house and on the farm. There was Christmas shopping to do and professional deadlines to meet. I wore myself into a rag-tag mess and collapsed into bed each night, only to wake the next morning and begin again.

Feed every living creature, hydrate, distribute meds, hydrate, take temperatures, hydrate, wash the laundry, hydrate, clean the house, change the sheets, disinfect everything, and feed the dog. Again. Oh, and hydrate!

By the fifth day, the house was on the mend, and spirits were on the rise. The zombies I lived with started to resemble people again. I was hopeful and happy with the results of my amped-up vitamin C intake.

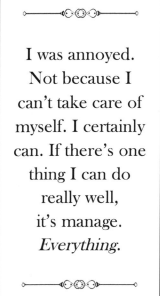

I was annoyed. Not because I can't take care of myself. I certainly can. If there's one thing I can do really well, it's manage. Everything.

Until I felt it. A gentle warning in the back of my throat quickly turned into an unmistakable throb. My head was pounding, and I was sneezing so often and so hard I thought my brains would shoot out of my eyeballs.

"It got me," I told my husband. "You're up," and I went to bed.

Now, I'll be honest—I'm not normally a whiner. I am certainly not as needy as these helpless creatures with whom I live. But it might have been nice for someone to say, "Honey, can I get you something? Here you go. No, no, no, let *me* clean this kitchen or do this laundry or rub your back or take your temperature or get you medicine or sing you a flipping lullaby."

But NO.

I got, "Hey, honey, I'm going to get the kids out of your hair for a while. Okay?"

I got bupkis with an extra dose of nada.

I was annoyed. Not because I can't take care of myself. I certainly can. If there's one thing I can do really well, it's manage. *Everything.* It was the principle of the matter, which states: "If you are newly recovered from a period of illness during which you were cared for and tended to by your loved one, and that loved one falls ill shortly thereafter, then you should return the favor if you find yourself able-bodied and capable of doing such a thing."

Instead, I got the vanishing act.

In truth, he thought he was helping. "I got the kids out of your hair!" he said. "I thought that would be a bigger help than anything else."

I get it. If I'm within a twenty-mile radius of my children, they will walk right past their father, who is sitting watching the Golf Channel, to find me clearly engaged in something important and ask me to open their snack bag of pretzels. But honestly? Sometimes I just want a little TLC all my own. To feel how I used to when my mom would make me a sick bed on the couch and bring over a TV tray stocked with a drink (hydrate!) and a bowl of soup.

I want my mom.

I want to go to my mom's house, walk in her front door, inhale her smell—a combination of Gain detergent, Chanel parfum, and freshly-baked cupcakes—and curl up on her couch. Or even in her bed with her. I want to stop adulting and let her take care of *me*.

She'll make her pot roast while I catch up on HGTV. I'll marvel at her as she effortlessly floats through the house like a fairy, whipping together meals with a flick of her wrist, no recipe in sight. I'll notice her knickknacks, carefully placed and thoroughly dusted. I'll notice how wherever she is still feels like home to me. She'll tuck in the covers around me and dim the lights as she says things like, "Oh, honey, you work too hard . . . Sweetie, you're doing a great job . . . You are a great mom." And I'll sigh, eat another cupcake, and say, "Yeah, you're right." Because I learned from the best, you see.

I try to emulate her—her culinary skills, her love, her talent for making a house a home. I try to create a space like hers, where the burdens on the shoulders of others fall to the floor at my threshold. Where my sniffly and sneezy children and husband can litter the whole place with their used tissues and empty Gatorade bottles while they watch episode after episode of *Teen Titans*.

But every now and then, and especially when the germs have tackled me to the ground, nobody in the home I make can make me feel at home.

Why?

Because I want my mom. She is *home* to me.

"The heart of a mother is a deep abyss at the bottom of which you will always find forgiveness."

—Honore de Balzac

23

BORED

by Melissa Rixon

I strutted through the door, totally stoked over the major accomplishment of actually getting to the gym. Demi Lovato's "Confident" blasted in my earbuds. My head bobbed in agreement. Yep, confident. I'd even slept in my workout clothes, just to be sure I wouldn't do that thing where I claim I can't find my workout pants. Poised and perched upon my high horse, I was ready to take on the day. Or at least a few sun salutations and a downward dog.

Standing around, waiting on the senior citizens to finish their chair fitness class, I struck up a conversation with a lady about her trendy yoga mat.

It was small talk at its best, which is a painful thing for me, but I persevered through all things weather, schedules, and protein powder before I went on about how crowded the gym always seems to be 9:30 a.m. when I assumed people should be at work.

She laughed and glanced at her watch and said, "Yeah, I don't have to been in the office until noon on Tuesdays. How about you?"

I sat there with my mouth agape like an idiot for what felt like twelve very long and awkward years, trying to think of a way to respond. My high horse bucked me off, then laughed in my face. The longer I paused, the more she seemed to stare at me and the more uncomfortable it all became.

I was supposed to have a job by now, I thought. *I was supposed to go back to work two years ago when my youngest went to kindergarten. It was sort of the deal.*

The deepest corners of my mind were erupting with accusations and excuses and questions and reflections. Alarms were sounding, and dams were breaking. There was a parade of people marching through it, holding picket signs that said things like "Lazy!" and "Loser!"

When I finally blinked it all away and refocused on that lady, she was still standing there, staring at me with a slight hint of concern on her face. So I, with all the self-loathing of an angsty teenager, blurted, "I don't have a job."

It wasn't even what I said, as much as how I said it, that's so embarrassing. Think of how you might tell someone you just peed your pants. That's how I said it. It was super.

I didn't explain. I didn't make up for it by listing any of the things I actually do—like work from home—because in my mind writing isn't a career. It's a hobby I hope to turn into a career one day. Yes, I manage a household of five, but that seems lame when you're staring at a perfect woman who is going to a probably perfect job at 12:00.

Now, ladies, before we go here, I want to make some things very clear. I have friends with jobs. I have friends without jobs. I have friends with part-time jobs and work-from-home jobs, flexible jobs and inflexible jobs, jobs that require travel and late nights and quick dinners and early mornings and skipped meals and all the stressful things. I am not here to divide us into camps of who does more and who sacrifices more and who loves their kids more and who will get the biggest crown in heaven, okay? That's so totally not my jam. I'm here to shed a little light on this question. On this . . . cultural divide.

Because as soon as I confessed—it felt like a confession, and that's a problem in itself—it was followed up with another question that felt ignorant and insulting and terribly insensitive, considering this woman had just watched me practically get a teenage period right in front of her.

A look of confusion wiggled into her eyes, and she asked, "Oh, wow, don't you get bored?"

This is where we're gonna get real. There is an invisible list of a million and one relentless things that keep me busy. I could rattle off the list to you now because I rattle it off frequently. Like when I'm melting down about feeling as if my life choices have been taken away—and were replaced with things I do with a pouty face. It consists of dishes and dinner and laundry and baseboards and grocery store running, actual running, dog walking, flower planting, plant watering and self-watering, friend helping, closet cleaning, toilet scrubbing, floor mopping, clothes ironing, drawer sorting, playroom disinfecting, and cleaning the otherworldly, sticky substance out of the microwave. Among a host of other things that, in isolation or in summary, can make me feel like my life took an unforeseen left turn into the land of drab.

But she didn't ask me what *I do*. I've been asked that before. It's the equivalent of asking a stay-at-home mother how they like their bonbons.

She asked me if I was *bored*.

Am I bad mom if I say *yes*?

To clean the same sink three times a day is boring. To have a sparkling shower and turn around to have a dirty shower in a matter of seven minutes is boring. To make one of the only three meals your entire family can agree upon is boring. This is where the name "bored housewife" comes from. It's not that there's nothing to do. It's that I'm an educated woman with brains and ambition, and some days I feel like I'm setting it aside to clean pee off toilet seats. It's the fact that there's not one iota of glamour in my day, unless I choose to be glamorous. Which would be stupid because vacuuming in heels in stupid. (I'm sorry, 1950s Housewife. It is. You knew this, surely.)

Well, mixed into this big, smelly pot of boredom is a flavor of something bitter, I'm afraid. I wish it wasn't easy to detect, but bitterness is a hard thing to hide.

Once upon a time, I was a professional in a real office where I crunched numbers and projected financials for a Fortune 500 company that sat firmly in the top fifty. I wore *heels*. I loved it. I was good at it! And I loved plotting my way up the ladder. Then I was an English teacher setting young minds on fire and helping them find purpose. Years later, when I was still dreaming of steering careers, my husband and I decided my temporary break from the workforce would benefit everybody. I struggled with it. Deeply struggled. The world was getting up and getting dressed and getting on with it . . . every day . . . while I was staying home and changing my shirt every time the baby spit up on me, until I grew so unmotivated I didn't even change that shirt anymore.

Too many dried spit-up shirts in a row will make you second-guess your own purpose in life. So I made another life choice and went back to work, where I rocked that out for all of three months before I sat on the edge of the bed with my head in my hands, dealing with the most blindsiding and mind-blowing fact of my life as I had known it.

Nobody tells you, before you have kids, that there will be no proper place for you. That staying home makes you long for work, and that working makes you long for staying home. I'd drop off my son, watch his face crumple into a wad of baby fat and then click-clack my heels across both of our hearts and the parking lot as I ran toward a day without diapers and pacifiers. In his very first preschool picture, he's recovering from pink eye and everything about his face says, "I want my mom." I buried that picture in the bottom of a drawer, somewhere my conscience would never have to see it. I struggled, for years, to find confidence in one decision one way or another; instead, I always felt like a flake.

> I'm reminded there used to be more to me than this relentless cycle of being nobody but everyone else's somebody.

After nearly ten years of being home, I'm pretty much used to the decision. But there's still an occasional encounter with someone like the lady in the gym. A moment where I'm reminded there used to be more to me than this relentless cycle of being nobody but everyone else's somebody.

Apparently, I'd totally spaced, contemplating this most piercing question, because when I came to, everyone was in class unrolling yoga mats and getting their initial hydrating sips of enhanced water. I almost walked in myself and unrolled my own mat in the middle of all the people stretching like cats and settling in their easy places in the world where they have labels and jobs that mean a thing or two more than pee-cleaner. I decided I needed a different view for the day. My own space with my own self and my own head and my own playlist of angry girl music. I walked to the treadmill and spent forty-five minutes burning it to the ground with all my insecurities lit like matches, one after another, to the relentless rhythm of my feet.

Then I felt better. Not found. No, I didn't feel found. There was no revelation. I didn't sort out all the questions and oozy feelings squirming into the front and center portion of my brain. I just came up with a response to a question. Which isn't an answer, but it's better than the avalanche of crazy that dumped all over everything when it caught me off guard.

I am bored. Yeah, I am. But I tell myself what I tell my kids when they're bored. It's not any person's responsibility and it certainly isn't life's job to entertain me. I am not a queen with an ordained purpose and a fool in my court to help me laugh if I need to. I am in charge of me and how I see myself and how I manage the life I've been given.

Sure, this life can get boring. But it's also blessed with choices. I'm not shackled to a kitchen or an office. I'm free to explore the possibilities hidden in both. Which I am doing. Day by day, word by written word, I'm exploring the possibilities of a career that doesn't look a thing like the one I studied for in college. Sometimes, I put it down to pick up a toilet brush. Sometimes, I put the toilet brush down to pick up a pen. The blessing is in choosing which and when.

I'm content to run to the rhythm of the choices that linger inside these days for now. Just crank up the beat, and I'll hop to it.

P.S. My husband would love it if I vacuumed in high heels. But it's still stupid.

TEMPER TANTRUM

"You never get me anything!"

Oh, child, I can't even. CANNOT EVEN with this one.

Nope, I never get you anything, do I?

Nothing. Ever, ever, ever, ever.

Especially the tub of M&M's® that is so deliberately

placed by the check-out lane.

So, you're right—I must not love you *at all*

because I've *never* gotten you *anything*.

24

TEARS OF JOY

by Teri Mirikitani

One of the most impactful memories I have of my son's younger years was when my husband, Jamie, was out of town for an extended period of time. At four years old, Nolan was missing his dad and seemed to be getting irritated with his father's absence. As a result, he started to give me little swats when he didn't like the decisions I made for him. I understood my sweet boy was struggling with his father's being away—so was I—but I was a parent who was determined to be consistent in correcting inappropriate behavior. And in my book, it was definitely inappropriate.

I could have easily ignored it. My boy was such a cuddlebug. He would give you the sweetest pats on your back with every hug. It was something he started when he was a barely more than one year old. These reassuring pats were so full of love. This, among many other things, such as his gentle and easygoing disposition, led me to believe his swatting me was not an issue of aggression. It was, however, a lesson in practicing self-control, and I was prepared to begin his education.

Repeatedly, I had explained the many reasons not to swat me, most of all how it hurt my feelings. I would say, "We hug with our hands" or "That makes Mommy sad" or "Use your words." He would nod in understanding and apologize for doing it and promise to try not to do it again. We'd hug it out, feel the love, and be hopeful for better execution the next time he disapproved of my decisions. I crossed my fingers.

This was tested one day when we were visiting Aunt Robin and Uncle Brent. We were saying our good-byes and, for a reason I've forgotten, he disagreed with me and gave me a swat. I immediately reminded him not to do this, giving him "the look" that had the power to stop him in his tracks. Evidently, not today. He didn't like my look of disapproval either, so he gave me another swat.

His usually calm, collected, and encouraging mother got down on his level, firmly grabbed him by the shoulders, looked him in the eyes, and said, "Don't you ever do that to me again." Every word was punctuated with the promise that he did not want me to dish out the consequences. All of this was in front of his aunt and uncle.

I slowly rose from my knees and looked in their direction to see their assessment of what they'd witnessed. I was relieved to see their almost unperceivable nods of approval. It was the nod that said, "We're 100 percent behind that decision. You're on the right track, Mom." I was relieved by their support.

I tried to move past our scene and on to our good-byes when I noticed my little angel wiping his eyes. He murmured, "Don't worry about me . . . these are tears of joy."

I looked to my sister-in-law, Robin, and we both strained to keep a straight face. He demonstrated quick wit in explaining away his tears. I made sure he did not see my reaction because I knew that he was embarrassed. It wasn't my intention to do this in front of an audience, but sometimes you can't wait to correct bad behavior, and I did so because we were among family who love him very much.

This was my first glimpse at a potential land mine. His obvious distress was a symptom of his fear of publicly messing up or making mistakes. I have always been so proud of what talents and skills came naturally to my children, but I also understand that the real work begins when things do not come naturally to them. At those times, it is my job to provide them with tools and skills to better handle a certain situation.

When Nolan started playing soccer, he loved the running, the kicking, and the strategy required to get the ball down the field and through the goal. He took to it like a duck to water. For him, it was a dream. Until the whistle blew. At some point, Nolan inadvertently touched the ball with his hand, and the coach blew the whistle to explain that at no point in soccer do you ever use your hands.

Nolan was startled. I sat in the stands and thought, *Oh no. This is not going to be good.* Nolan started walking off the field, gently wiping his eyes, saying, "These allergies are killing me." Once again, my sweet boy couldn't shake off the suffocating feeling that he messed up royally.

This hypersensitivity to making mistakes was the symptom of his weakness. It was "go time" for me and Jamie. We were dedicated to arming him with the abilities to figure out how to diffuse this feeling in the future. The truth is, it's troubling how we are taught at such a young age to cover up our emotions, mistakes, and failures. We are prepared to do anything except be vulnerable. It's sad because our emotions are what give our lives color, dimension, and depth. It's the human element that makes life rich, and vulnerability is part of the package that comes when we challenge ourselves. We are not born with all the answers. We will make mistakes so that we can learn to better handle our own emotions and our reactions to the emotions of others. All the great success stories are laced with failures before achievements were reached.

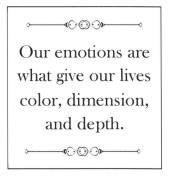

Our emotions are what give our lives color, dimension, and depth.

Kids are resilient, so they'll stick to what they know and resist the uncomfortable. Who doesn't? But our kids need our guidance and tips and tools in order to process the things that challenge them. It's not a quick fix or one-size-fits-all formula for success. It's a long process full of successful days and times of failure.

We were committed to helping Nolan by sharing our observations, providing feedback, and hopefully suggesting some tools to try. But we were not prepared for the resistance. And, oh my, was there some resistance! Gently pointing out an opportunity to consider a new approach brought frustration and fueled his shame. His old behavior was like an impenetrable piece of armor that sometimes was so strong, it wore us down. It was in this moment I realized that Nolan's biggest weakness was also a catalyst that helped him. The paradox was that he was determined not to be embarrassed and so was driven to succeed, which helped him enjoy much success in school and sports. It was a delicate balance. We didn't want to destroy what challenged him, because it also gave him the fire to succeed—which is also an important element to not only surviving but also thriving in life.

This certainly reconfirmed our dedication to helping our son figure out the balance of having a strong drive to succeed and having no embarrassment in failure. Failures are only results, pushing us to change the input in order to obtain a different output. It's our choice.

The big lesson I learned from my son? We are all born with strengths and weaknesses, and it's our paths to march on trying, failing, learning, and trying again. You will feel raw and exposed, but that vulnerability is part of the risk that leads to the reward.

It doesn't end in childhood. Exploring new ideas stimulates us and renews us throughout our lives. This was something Christi, Melissa, and I grappled with when writing this book. Could we do it? Should we do it? The alternative was playing it safe and staying within our comfort zones. But that is the path to boredom and stagnation. Who wants a life like that? Not the three of us. And so, sitting in that little café that day, the three of us said, "Let's go for it." Sure, we were scared to death. Putting yourself out there like a flashing neon sign is risky. What if we're laughed at? Ridiculed? Shunned? What if our words didn't make sense to anybody else? What if we . . . failed?

But what if we didn't fail? What if we actually tried something new, learned from it, and *enjoyed* it? And what if we actually succeeded? We'd never know unless we took that first bold step. Doing so, we learned that being vulnerable is tough at times. Very tough. But the rewards? Oh, the rewards along the journey have already been so worth it.

If the tears must fall, let them be tears of joy to celebrate our courage in pushing our boundaries. To see just what we're capable of achieving. Tears of joy in learning about life. And tears of joy in learning about ourselves.

TERI'S MOTHERHOOD RESUME

Look what I can do . . .

- Make lemonade when handed lemons in life and laugh about it.
- Give pedicures and manicures for all family members.
- Clean horse stalls and tack.
- Train polo ponies and drive cross-country with a twelve-horse trailer.
- Turn off lights and close blinds. Every. Single. Night.
- Remind everyone of morning routine. And bedtime routine.
- Alter one meal four different ways.
- Repair a sad heart.
- Talk with pretty much anyone, anywhere, even in bad Spanish.
- Help my children forgive mean people.
- Spray stinky soccer cleats.
- Hang up wet bath and pool towels.
- Remind hubby it's trash night.
- Walk the dog. Feed the dog. Groom the dog.
- Morph into the world's best baseball catcher for my son's pitching practice in the yard.
- Repair any clogged drain.
- Cheer for everyone's kid at baseball and soccer.

"The best part of being a mom to me is the unconditional love. I have never felt a love as pure, a love that's as rewarding."

—Monica Denise Brown

25

I AM RICH

by Christi McGuire

I sat in church, fighting that I've-not-had-my-coffee-yet-and-I-barely-made-it-to-church-on-time state of mind, when my pastor stood at the pulpit and exclaimed, "I am RICH!" He paused for dramatic effect while the congregation was jolted out of our comas, waiting for him to share more. He went on to explain that he considers himself to be rich based on the number of meaningful and authentic friendships he has. "If that is a true measure of wealth, then I am the richest man alive," he said.

I've been around long enough to have had relationships with all types of people. Some have left me feeling happy and incredibly fulfilled. While, truthfully, others have left me feeling picked clean. I began taking stock of my own friendships, both past and present, and I found this example of wealth to be profoundly meaningful.

There are friends who I've identified as my start-up investors. The ones who were there during the lonely years of raising babies and toddlers. We'd have Tuesday morning playdates and sip coffee while our kiddos crushed goldfish into the carpet. We'd talk over the cacophony of noise as the little ones would turn on all the toys that beeped, talked, or played music. We'd somehow hold conversations while we simultaneous steered toddlers by the shoulders, out of the way of nasty falls or things they may be tempted to stick in their mouths. We'd cry out of confusion, frustration, or sheer exhaustion. We'd laugh at the hilarity of it all. And we'd leave with charged batteries, ready to tackle the business end of motherhood again until the next Tuesday morning.

Our kids are older now, caught in the machine of obligations and activities, and we no longer have playdates and morning chats in noisy living rooms. But I still treasure those ladies who kept me sane when that was such a hard thing to do.

Other friends are scattered across the country. The ones I've collected over the expanse of a lifetime. My long-term investors. They're the ones I rarely see outside of Facebook, but when we do get together we laugh at the history and the stories buried in it. No matter the distance or time between visits, we can happily pick it up exactly where we left it. Tried, true, and there for the duration, they keep me in good fortune now and forever.

And then there's my gold mine. The ones I call *Tribe*. The ones who keep me stable from day-to-day, hour-to-hour, and minute-to-minute. The ones I'd call at 3 a.m. The ones I hope call me at 3 a.m.

But there's one character that will creep in if we aren't careful. If we aren't on guard, there are those who always make withdrawals. Ones who never give back much of themselves. Take advantage of whatever someone is willing to give. They take all the favors, but never offer one in return. They never fill us up. They discourage us. Suck us dry and soak us into their negativity. We have to be careful because these people will cost us time and energy and deplete our relationship bank accounts. A financial drain like that can be especially detrimental because it can cost you so many other opportunities for wealth and enrichment!

If we hope to feel the fullness of joy within our lives and our relationships, then we need to value those friendships that add value. And we need to peacefully set free those relationships that drag us into the red.

Only then can we exclaim, "I am rich—I have wonderful friends and my investments are sound."

What a beautiful gift to claim!

TEMPER TANTRUM

Yes, I know it's the most unfair thing *ever* that you should have to unload the dishwasher that I loaded with dishes that were dirty from the meals I cooked with groceries I bought with the money I made.

26

LICE IN MY BRAIN

by Melissa Rixon

I hosted my daughter's birthday tea party, a bright and gaudy affair full of oversized flowers, tiny sandwiches, and intentionally mismatched tea cups. I decorated the table with about a hundred colorful brooches from my mother's collection. We had a miniature lesson in etiquette. There was a bouquet of edible fruit and enough chicken salad to feed the 114th Congress. Queen Elizabeth herself would have been proud of my attempt to give these seven-year-old little girls a memorable day of good taste and the fixings of a proper tea. After three hours of eating sugar cubes whole (with pinkies up), I sent the girls on their merry ways back to their homes to speak of crumpets and scones with clotted cream.

The next morning, I went to Target to pick up the supplies for my son's birthday party—to be held that afternoon. (At this moment I will insert a mini-lecture on the importance of sound family planning. If you do not practice such a thing you could end up with two children born in the same month and one child born at Christmas. Them's just the breaks.)

While I was racing about grabbing party favors and odds and ends, I received a frantic phone call from one of the mothers whose daughter had been at my house for tea. "Emily has lice," she said. "I hate to drop that panic bomb on you, but I knew I should tell you, and you might want to spread the word."

Panic? Yes. I certainly felt that. Wanting to spread the word? No. I did not feel that at all. I felt dread. I felt the need to change our names and enter into a witness protection program. Did I send those little ladies home with paper fans, petit fours, and cooties?

All the way home I imagined bugs crawling in every crevice of my house, in every stitch of fabric, on every stuffed animal, and even in the pillbox hats we'd made. Then I blacked out and somehow arrived home with two plastic bags full of the poison in which people willingly soak themselves when bugs move into our heads. I flew inside like a tornado.

"Go stand in the light, Madeline!" I yelled, slinging bags on the counter and rolling up my sleeves. "Does your head itch? Have you felt anything crawling around?"

She was rightfully startled. I was rightfully freaking out. And it only got worse when I discovered them. Eggs and eggs and eggs, and bugs and bugs and bugs. Living on her scalp. Just living there. Thriving there. Multiplying there. I had no idea how long this had been going on. From the looks of things, they'd already colonized and elected a town council, so I assumed it had been some time.

"Didn't you feel this?" I shrieked. "Why didn't you say anything? You were itching, weren't you?" Just writing this, I am itching. Just writing this makes me want to poison my head again, actually.

I called for the boys and checked and then rechecked to find nothing living in their heads, thank God Almighty. "I have to get to this house before I can work through your hair," I said. And I put Madeline away in hiding.

A quick glance at the clock . . . I had three hours. Three hours to delouse my house before a dozen eight-year-old boys descended on it for a day of gaming and pizza. I sprayed and spritzed poison all around like a happy homemaker spraying springtime air freshener. I bagged up anything in the house that even seemed remotely inviting for a louse to call home. I diligently called, e-mailed, and texted each mother of each girl who could have brought home the worst party favor ever and told them the news that makes every mother quake with horror and disgust. Then I e-mailed her teacher. I sprayed and vacuumed and mopped and sprayed some more, and then I had a party with my daughter safely in quarantine.

It was quite the day.

When the party was over, we spent three hours picking eggs and dead bugs out of her hair.

In a word . . . daymare. Which is a nightmare that happens in the middle of the day while the sunlight illuminates your daughter's head lice. Moms, if you've been through this, you know what I'm talking about. If you haven't . . . just you wait.

It took three hours and cost me fifty dollars in chemical warfare, a good kink in my neck, and a bonus of upper-back pain, but I was confident it was well taken care of. I took all the bedding off every single bed and threw it in the garage. I took every thread of clothing from her bedroom and tossed it out there with it. I was a giant fighting an infinitesimal army, and I was relentless and overwhelming.

But it takes more than being unrelenting to beat lice. I learned this three weeks later when they returned with a vengeance, and a few were giving me the middle finger. I looked around my house in horror.

Three weeks they've been here without my knowing, I thought. *I've sat there. I've laid down in her bed to read. Rolled around with the dog on that rug. She slept on my pillow. I may have used her hairbrush.*

Suddenly, I felt them. I had it too.

Didn't I do everything I was supposed to do?

I read the directions on all that poison again. And there, in plain print, was the bit of instruction I'd apparently missed. "Repeat this process in seven to ten days."

I dug at my own head until I nearly drew blood. "I. have. it!" I screeched at my husband as he searched my hair for the invisible devils. "You're missing something. I FEEL them crawling around on my head!" I said. And each time he dug through my hair, he came up empty-handed.

"There's nothing, Melissa," he said. "I don't see a thing."

"That's because you don't see anything!" I yelled. "You can't find the milk when it's the biggest, most obvious thing in the refrigerator! How are you going to find something that has EVOLVED in order to stay hidden?"

I asked my mother to check me, but she didn't trust her own eyesight.

I asked my sister, but she wouldn't come near me. "They don't jump," I told her. "I learned that on the Internet. I also know all about their mating patterns and stages of development, if you care to know."

"They tell you they don't jump because they're trying to avoid mass hysteria," she said. "It's sort of like how they probably won't tell us if an asteroid is on course to blow up the earth. It's better if everyone stays calm." And so she calmly *stayed away from me.*

As luck would have it, I stared into the distance, forlorn and depressed and about to call the "lice fairies," who are actual people who make a living delousing families, when my hairdresser called to confirm my appointment for the next morning.

"I'm sorry, Haai," I said. "I hate to cancel, but we just found out my daughter has head lice. I don't want to come in until I'm sure I don't have it too."

Oh, my sweet, teeny-tiny, Cantonese, firecracker of a hairdresser. God love her and her fierce personality.

"You come in," she insisted. "We kill your lice."

"Are you . . . sure?" I asked. "I don't want to spread it. It's embarrassing!" My raw, desperate emotion was pouring forth at this point.

"No. Do not be embarrassed," she spouted. "Come in now. I take care of it for you."

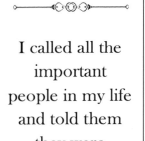

> I called all the important people in my life and told them they were demoted and I was changing my will to leave everything to my hairdresser.

So I called all the important people in my life and told them they were demoted and I was changing my will to leave everything to my hairdresser— the only person in the world who cared enough to do battle for me.

I walked into her salon with a stew of humility, gratitude, and anxiety simmering inside me. I sat down in her chair, both hopeful and doubtful, while she mixed the solution she uses to color my hair—as if it was any other day of the week. Then, with a certain flinty look in her eye, a clenched jaw, and bit of anger in her voice, she seethed, "I suffocate your lice."

I imagined the tiny bugs screaming, grabbing their young, and running to hide in their villages, escaping the rushing waves of the goldenrod, chemically-laden goo she vigorously and aggressively squirted and massaged into my head.

When it was entirely coated, we waited. She rinsed it. She blew it dry. I was feeling confident. She seemed calm and collected and in control. Then, with all the grit and determination of a true superhero, she pulled out a flat iron and growled, "Your lice not survive four hundred degrees. We burn them."

It was amazing. I was so scared and so happy she was on my team. After thirty minutes of taking tiny sections of hair and scorching them slowly and methodically, I was finished. I looked good. I felt good. I was ready to take on the world again, but I feared it wasn't over.

"Don't I need to go through it with one of those little combs? I will pay you extra to do that. I have nobody else I can trust!"

She smiled. "You don't have lice," she said.

I was almost suspicious.

"Are you serious?" I asked "I was sure I did!"

"No. You have lice in your brain." She laughed, poking me in the forehead. "Your mind can make you think anything is real. But you should flat iron your daughter's hair."

I went back home, glammed up with my fresh new 'do, and waged a war, yet again, on the tiny visitors lurking in the microscopic depths. I doused and combed and fired up the flat iron, then tackled my own daughter's hair with the same clenched jaw and determination I'd learned from Haai. And I thanked God for tiny warrior women. The ones who give us knowledge and stamina and set examples of what it means to fight and, at the end of the day, give us the tools to win.

I haven't seen a louse since.

TEMPER TANTRUM

Toy Packaging = A glass of wine, a chainsaw, and a probable trip to the ER. Always have 911 on standby when opening a new Barbie doll.

27

COMING FULL CIRCLE

by Teri Mirikitani

How is a mom born? Is it when she realizes she's pregnant, seeing the first ultrasound picture of her expected child, or when she decorates the nursery and buys baby clothes, or holds the newborn in her arms? Are we born as moms? Are we born with the seed of motherhood already within us, and time is the fertilizer that helps it grow until it's ready to bloom?

If I reflect on my childhood days, I loved "playing mommy." With some toys from my closet and odds and ends I'd swipe from the kitchen, I'd set the stage in a pretend house while I'd feed and change my dolls a few times before moving on to blocks, crayons, or cartoons. It's as if that seed of motherhood was already within me, and time *was* the fertilizer that helped it grow and blossom into the two little people I now call son and daughter.

When my daughter, Alise, was born, I remained firmly in the middle of awe and panic as I witnessed all the many firsts of my firstborn. Rolling over, sitting up, chewing on first words like big wads of bubble gum, and walking. Oh, the walking! What a moment for the video camera, those first steps. Wobbly and proud and highlighted with a surprised smile on both her and me.

And then, within moments, the gravity of a walking baby sets in. It meant there was no more relaxing, only the full-time job of chasing, chasing, chasing while I waited on cognition to get a handle on her and relieve me of the overwhelming responsibility to keep her busy body from getting hurt. Or worse. Hanging on to the promise of naptime got me through the mornings. And the promise of bedtime, through the afternoon.

She'd go to sleep, and so would I. Both exhausted and spilled out, we'd rest in the delight of each other. But there were moments I'd just stare at her and freak out. *Am I getting this right? Is this how you do this?*

There is no all-inclusive handbook on motherhood, and while sometimes I think that's a good thing, there were so many moments I could have used one. Instead, I'd call my big sister, Amy. She was a veteran mom and one I admired, so I'd pick advice from her like apples. Ripe and shiny and there for the taking. "I'm afraid I messed it all up today," I'd say. She'd ask me how or why, and I'd carry on about maybe buying the wrong baby soap or not making my own baby food like another mom I met last week.

Amy turned out to be my Guardian Mom. The one with the gentle words of encouragement and the pats on the back. The one to make it all okay and ultimately make me believe in myself. That I could do this job without training because I had instincts.

> Your love for
> your baby is
> what makes
> you perfect.

"Your love for your baby is what makes you perfect," she told me. It was the way she said it that made me believe it. Her voice was strong and convincing. With tears in my eyes, I listened: "You are perfect for her," she said.

I would never have survived those first shaky moments of motherhood without Amy.

When baby Nolan made us a family of four, I watched my daughter step into her own big sisterly role. She wanted to hold him, cover him with his blankie, and tend to his little cries. As he grew older, she grew deeper into her role, enthusiastically leading him in his daily routines, showing him just how much toothpaste to put on the toothbrush and how to clock the time by singing the ABCs. "Open wide like this!" she'd model, as I flossed his tiny teeth.

At mealtimes, she'd offer advice on how to hold his fork and where to place his napkin. How to sit nicely and show good manners. "Say please and thank you," she'd remind him while coaching him through the sibling challenges of sharing and taking turns. He'd take his orders and say his pleases and thank-yous, and she'd look on with satisfied approval.

I would look at her in these moments and wonder, *What awaits you? What kind life will you lead? What kind of woman will you become? Will you be kind and helpful all your life?* I've caught glimpses of these promises in her so many times over the years.

It was on display one evening, when my mother was visiting. My husband, Jamie, and I were enjoying a rare night out. On a sunset walk with Alise and the dog, my mother took stock of things and said, "You know, Alise, we should be getting back. I think it's going to get dark soon."

Alise looked up with her big, brown eyes, convinced her grandma was scared. "Don't worry, Mema!" she said. "I'll hold your hand!"

It was again on display on a later visit when my mother took a wrong turn directly into a traffic jam. Alise piped in from the back seat, "Don't worry Mema! Everyone makes mistakes!"

These moments . . . are they promises? Are they the slow unfolding of a mother being born? Is this how I used to be? And my mother before me?

As the years have passed, I've continued to watch as my little girl soaks us all in her love and encouragement. She was the card maker at birthdays, Mother's Day, and Father's Day and the party decorator of walls and tables papered in homemade signs and crafts. She would lead us into the room with a loud "Ta-da!" and watch as we took in the festive evidence of a girl who loved us and loved being happy. With her eyes sparkling like diamonds and a giant smile spread across her face, she gifted us over and over again with herself.

She learned to make me coffee, just how I liked it, and still loves to surprise me with a morning cup of decaf. The first time she made it for me, my eyes welled with tears, and I was overcome with the feeling of being cherished by my child. A love so pure and unconditional, it took my breath away.

She's coming into the teen years, and I'm still watching as this sweetness in her nature continues to bloom. Now she spreads her kindness to her friends, encouraging them to be happy and try their best, and she genuinely celebrates them when they do. She's a pleasant presence wherever she may be.

She needs me less and less, and I know that's just life. That's par for the course as moms. But what a joy to watch your daughter fulfill her own destiny, as time fertilizes the seeds within her, as they did in me.

Watching my daughter and all of the beautiful girls around the world carry the essence of a mother reaffirms my belief that the wondrous qualities of motherhood are a gift. And this love and compassion is the thread of humanity the world cannot live without.

Indeed, we all come full circle.

"Being a mom has made me so tired. And so happy."

—Tina Fey

28

WHAT IS MOTHERHOOD?

Sometimes it's the feeling of being too full and too empty all at once.

Always there but maybe never good enough.

All out of time and giving more of it for free.

Kicking yourself for missed opportunities today, swearing them off for tomorrow, and waking to miss opportunities again.

It's striving so hard to be perfect but forgetting you're good enough.

It's taking that chair closest to the kitchen, so you can get up and down at dinner.

Eating the rubbery macaroni and cheese in the bottom of the pot, or a cold steak in a restaurant, or sipping microwaved coffee. Again.

It's a constant gratitude for healthy children, a fear that won't always be the case, and an ache in your heart for those who aren't so lucky.

Going without pie because there wasn't enough.

A bath, with an audience.

A phone conversation in front a parade.

It's breaking fevers and fixing boo-boos.

Holding chewed bubble gum and dirty socks and boogers.

Reading Dr. Seuss with your eyes closed.

Listening to hurt feelings with your heart open.

It's trying harder at something than you have in your whole life, and then feeling the guilt of wondering why you never tried that hard at a career—and if you did, then where would you be?

It's thinking of that girl. The one with the career on fire and the clothes and the figure and the money and status—all while you look in the mirror at who you are instead and grapple with whether you can be proud of her.

It is never knowing if you're doing the right thing, lamenting every decision you've already made, and swearing to make a better one next time, knowing deep down you'll fail a hundred more times. By tomorrow.

It's bleeding dry. Financially, physically, emotionally, mentally— every minute of every day for the whole of a lifetime.

It's knowing that even when there's nothing left of you but bones, you lay them at the feet of someone who could use them up.

It's seeing every child as your own.

It's weeping for moms on hard times.

It's weathered knees from fervent prayers.

It's an aching back from heavy loads.

It's passing down recipes, remedies, and relics.

It's teaching and learning. And teaching what you learn.

It's making a home and playing house and smiling at the difference between the two.

It's standing on your feet for three days in the kitchen to make a holiday meal that's eaten in minutes.

It's cleaning that kitchen for two more hours as the masses who ate your turkey sleep it off on the couches.

And it's looking out . . . over those dreaming faces, smiling at their full tummies, knowing they're satisfied and that *you did that*. Because ultimately that is what motherhood is. It's *filling people up*. With food and well wishes and prayers and "atta boys." With advice and strong counsel, spines of steel, honest eyes, sensitive hearts, and trusted guts. With Scripture verses and good examples, vitamins and hearty breakfasts. It's filling their minds with positive thoughts, wise proverbs, and recollections to see them through when you're not around.

Because motherhood is eventually *bowing out.*

It's standing back and trusting that all you did, both good and bad, will filter. And the wasted opportunities and mistakes and failures that clotted each day will be sifted out.

It's the hope that all you ever did that was good and well intending, those moments when you were a woman on fire and right there with the right things to say and a sturdy hug, will stoke the flame in the torch you pass on. The one still alive with the fire your mother passed to you, and hers to her, and hers to her.

What is motherhood?

It is the great spreading and sharing of light.

EPILOGUE

Dear Fellow Mommy,

Thank you for joining this journey with us—for reading our stories, listening to our hearts, and sharing in this amazing odyssey of motherhood. We hope you've laughed, perhaps cried, but most of all thought, "ME TOO!"

At times we may joke and whine and complain about being a mom and about our kids and our husbands. This is a safe place to do just that. But at the end of the day, albeit exhausted and harried and flicking off baby spit-up from our shirts that we've been wearing for three days in a row, we love our lives. We love our kiddos, our hubbies, and the season we're in (or at least we're trying to). Because we know that all too soon, it'll be gone. Over. In a flash. Blink and the kids are out of the house, and we get to do all the things we want to do without having to cut up a little person's food or wipe someone else's butt. And by then, we know, we'll be in mourning. We'll wish for these days back. The days of driving six giggly girls to volleyball practice. Of scurrying to the Halloween party at school because the Room Mom (darn her!) signed us up to bring the Monster Munchies. Of not being able to reserve a party of one to pee. Of kissing the boo-boos, wiping the noses, and saying the prayers at bedtime. Of hearing, "Mommy!" 1,572 times a day.

We will miss this. But while we're in the trenches, it's okay to reach out to your fellow soldier, give her a hug, and say, "Hang in there!" It's okay to have a temper tantrum at age forty. It's a fleeting moment, but it's also a necessary moment.

Above all, we want you to remember that you do get a turn. You *deserve* a turn. Maybe you can't take it today. Maybe you'll have to schedule it—ten minutes here or five minutes there. But you are worthy of a turn.

And Mom? You're doing a great job. You are awesome!

Your Fellow Mamas,
Christi, Melissa, and Teri

ACKNOWLEDGMENTS

Melissa, Christi, and Teri would like to thank . . .

- Our husbands, for their endless support and encouragement, their willingness to read more estrogen-filled words than any men ever should, and their ability to hold down the forts, fix thrown-together meals, dig clean, unfolded clothes out of laundry baskets, overlook the dancing dust bunnies, and take care of kiddos when the Big Magic of writing took over.
- Our kids, Michael, Madeline, Merrick, Mary-Allison, Mia, Alise, and Nolan, for being our biggest cheerleaders. What amazingly smart, talented, caring, and kind children you are! We hope we've paved a path of courage for you to pursue your own dreams.
- Our moms, who rocked out motherhood in the 1970s and 80s. We're not sure how you did it, since you didn't have Facebook or Pinterest to tell you how to reuse Mason jars or that you should pack Bento lunches for us. You didn't even have Instagram to post those blurry pictures of us in frilly Easter dresses and saddle shoes. Somehow you made it through, and you're the reasons we wanted to become mamas ourselves. Every day is a tribute to you, and we thank you. We only hope our own kiddos look up to us half as much as we do you.
- Adelle Gabrielson, our editor, who was brave enough to give it to us straight, knowing that the end product would be something moms needed. You were an invaluable resource. What a gift you have, and what a privilege to have you sprinkle it on us! We are forever grateful and indebted to you.
- Brianna Hilvety, our cover designer, who took Melissa's illustration and our crazy ideas and wrapped them together to create a beautiful package.
- Our friends, who embrace us and our hair-brained ideas. Who are in the trenches with us, giving 200 percent effort every single day as moms. Who need a break, a laugh, and a turn.

ABOUT THE AUTHORS

Christi McGuire has worked in the publishing industry as a freelance editor, writer, and consultant for sixteen years. She has published more than one hundred magazine articles and dozens of children's devotionals and curricula. Christi is co-founder and co-owner of the Christian Editor Network LLC and is the director of two of its divisions: Christian Editor Connection, an organization that connects authors with freelance editors, and The PEN Institute, an online, educational institute for Christian editors. She lives in Bradenton, Florida, with her husband, Matt, and their two daughters, Mary-Allison and Mia. Visit her website at www.ChristiMcGuire.com.

Melissa Rixon is a novelist with degrees in both English and Communications Science and Disorders from the University of South Florida. She married her love of language and children by teaching secondary English and pursuing speech language therapy. Her lifelong passion is writing for women, and she does so from her home in Sarasota, Florida. She and her husband, Matt, have three children who drive them to continue learning, setting new goals, and finding inspiration in the everyday corners of life. Her next project is a stand-alone novel, due out in 2018.

Teri Mirikitani is a certified life coach and blogger. She also trains horses for her husband's professional polo career. Earning a BS in both Business and Psychology from the University of Pittsburgh, she has spent her adult life helping people reach their personal and professional goals. Teri lives in Sarasota, Florida, with her husband, Jamie, and their two children, Alise and Nolan. She strives to empower people with tools for success and passion to achieve their goals. You can find Teri's messages of self-reflection and positivity on JustTeri.com.

READING DISCUSSION QUESTIONS

Do you belong to a book club? Check out the reading discussion questions for book clubs on our website, *www.WhensItMyTurn.com.*

Invite the authors to your book club!
E-mail Melissa, Christi, and Teri at
WhensItMyTurnBook@gmail.com.

Tri Solutions LLC is a company that supports and encourages women. Stay tuned for future book releases and events from Tri Solutions LLC.